RENEW YOUR MIND

RENEW YOUR MIND

with

Joy
Experience
Success
Understanding
Sanity

PUBLISHING CO., INC.
P.O. BOX 3117
BATON ROUGE, LA 70821

Quotes from the King James Bible and The Amplified Bible.

TABLE OF CONTENTS

CHARTS

Acknowledgement

I wish to thank my good friend, Jay Campagna, for prodding me continuously to write this book after I finished teaching the material it contains to a Bible study group in his home; I want to thank my wife for typing and retyping the transcript. A deep, heartfelt thanks goes to my wife's sister, Mrs. Carol Adams, of Akron, Ohio for the long hours she spent in editing the manuscript.

Introduction

On July 16, 1952, I was a country boy who had just turned 16, all 6'3" and 210 pounds of me — a sharecropper's son with a lot of problems that came to a head that hot day in July. Some of them went back to the early days of my parents' marriage — before I was even born. Others had accumulated during the first 16 years of my life. The carefree country boy was anything but what he seemed.

Part of the problem, I'm sure, was the quick-tempered ethnic heritage of my folks. My mother was black Dutch and Irish. My father was almost full-blood Cherokee Indian and one of the meanest men who ever lived.

In the early days after he and mama were married, they had come home from a trip to town and found a strange man sitting at their table eating cornbread and syrup. They hadn't locked the door when they left that morning — country folks didn't do that and anyhow they didn't have anything worth stealing.

When he saw them coming, the stranger ran out of the house and started across the field. My dad sent the dog after him. He made it about halfway across the field before daddy reached the woodpile and took hold of his ax. He went into the field after that man, hit him with the ax, and killed him.

The hot-tempered couple lit a long-lasting burner in their early years, and it was one on which I would simmer for many long months. And years. Some folks say having a baby helps a marriage...but all five of us "young-uns" didn't help mama and daddy. In my earliest memory, daddy woke us kids up in the middle of the night to tell us goodbye. He had been seeing one of mama's nieces; mama had found out about it and she was mad. She'd been crying and the two of them had been fussin' most of the night.

Daddy owned two pairs of overalls; he was wearing one pair and had the other pair rolled up under his arm. He got us up before he left to tell us goodbye. I was just a little boy and I was scared to think daddy was leaving and I would never see him again. He was mean some-times...but he was the only daddy I had and I couldn't imagine what life would be like without him.

We started to cry, almost all at the same time, and he got mad. He started fussing at <u>us</u>, then, threatening to "beat the devil out of you-all," and made us go back to bed. The next thing we knew, he tossed his rolled-up overalls in a chair, pulled off his other pair, and him and mama went back to bed and went to sleep. He was still there in the morning. This scene was repeated over and over, with few changes in it, until mama died in 1970.

I grew up in north central Louisiana where there was an abundance of tall, rich pine timber. Around the turn of this century, the Bienville Lumber Company had cut a lot of virgin pine. Wherever they left tree tops and stumps, the resin had preserved this part of the tree and made it excellent kindling wood for our heating and cooking stoves.

Winter time had come, it was very cold, and we were out of kindling. Daddy and I hitched our team of a grey horse and grey mule to the old wagon and went way back in the piney woods looking for kindling. When we got the wagon loaded, the horse decided he didn't want to pull it home. Daddy tried whipping him with a bull whip he always kept handy. But the horse wouldn't go.

When this didn't work, he cut a big hickory pole about 6' long and beat the horse with it. The horse still wouldn't budge. Daddy took a pine log off the wagon, chopped it up, piled it under the horse, and set it on fire. Before long the horse decided he wanted to pull that wagon, but then daddy wouldn't let him go. He made the horse stand in the fire as long as he could. It seemed the poor animal was almost cooked. I couldn't stand to see him treat the horse like that, and I started to cry and beg daddy not to burn him alive. He told me to shut up or he would use the hickory club on me.

I was ten years old at the time and I shut up. I knew he meant it. He'd beaten me many times with his bull whip. I didn't dare test him to see whether he'd use the hickory club on me. I knew he would. This was just one more day to get through — one more exercise in avoiding his wrath.

For 16 years life went on the same. My dad went from one affair to another. He beat us, criticized us, and condemned everything we did. It seemed we could never do anything right. Sometimes mama fought back and sometimes she didn't...but she had all she could do to hold herself together. She couldn't fight him for us too.

I grew up thinking I was worthless, unlovable, unforgivable, and that there was no hope of changing. I felt that surely he must be right — after all, he was the parent and I was the child.

And then my world caved in. I couldn't take any more. I couldn't eat or sleep. I couldn't rest. Like the demoniac of Gadara who lived among the tombs, I walked the woods day and night — roaming the trails animals had made...but with one difference. They were at home. I felt hopelessly lost.

In 30 days I lost 45 pounds. I thought I had sinned against God and was eternally lost; that I would never hear the voice of God speak to me again. It was as if every devil in hell had come to get my soul and drag me into the bottomless pit.

That's a big load for a 16-year-old boy to carry alone. I didn't realize at the time that children transfer the way they believe their <u>parents</u> feel about them into their understanding of God...and somehow they think <u>God</u> feels the same way about them as their <u>parents</u> do. I carried that burden for many years until I learned God's prescription for transferring it from my shoulders to His.

I had accepted Christ as my Saviour three years earlier, at the age of 13. But I wasn't mature enough in the Lord at 16 to know how He longed to carry this load for me. I thought I had to carry it for myself. And I couldn't leave home — I knew I had to stay there, finish high school, and wait for the right time. I prayed it would be soon.

How patiently did the Lord work with me during the next 11 long, dark, tormenting years! He taught me how to deal with the problems of life; how to apply His Word to my daily living; how to make it work for me in my relationship to Him, to the world around me, to the Church, and most important of all, how to make His Word work for me in my relationship to my own self. I learned how much He loves me — and what that love empowers me to be and do in His name.

The years from 16 to 27 covered a lifetime's worth of learning and growing in God for me. That is what this book is all about. While it is simple in nature, that simplicity is eloquent when it brings the things of God close and clear. It is as carefully balanced against Scripture as I can make it — and therein lies any claim to excellence.

Through the studies that follow, I pray God's Word will come clear to you in a way it never has before, light a warm fire of hope in your heart, and help you reach out to someone else in our world who needs to hear!

At the back of this book are five charts which will be referred to in the following chapters.

Below is an explanation of Chart #1 found on page 104. Please examine the chart and get a picture of it in your mind before you read the explanation.

The outer circle represents the fleshly, carnal man who is ruled by his five senses: touch, taste, smell, sight, and sound. Feeling is the voice of the carnal man. His philosophy is, "If it feels good, do it." The carnal man seeks to control your life and mine.

The second circle represents the natural, soulish man: your mind, your intellect, or personality. He tries to explain every-thing through reason. Since reason is his voice, faith cannot operate when he is in control. The natural man wants to control your life and mine.

Finally, the inner circle represents the spirit man, whose voice is conscience. The shaded gray area inside this circle repre-sents the Holy Spirit, who abides in every spirit-filled Christian. He is the voice of God. He speaks to your heart. He wants to restore the controls of your life and mine to the only one who has legitimate claims to them.

Keep this in mind, because we'll come back to it later. For this moment, realize there are three forces at work for control of your life.

Chapter 1
"In the beginning..."

Somewhere in eternity past, when Lucifer became puffed up and his heart filled with pride, he was stripped of the power and authority God had given him except for one small area of the universe. Earth. Lucifer was the brightest, most intelligent, most beautiful creature God had ever created.

Of all the created beings in heaven — angels, archangels, seraphim, and cherubim — Lucifer ranked highest. Some theologians believe Lucifer was an archangel, but he wasn't. Their rank was different from his, and their purposes were different from his.

When God created the angels, He created them in three groups, for three different purposes.

The first group was the Messenger Angels; Gabriel was given charge over them. In *Luke Chapter 1,* Gabriel the archangel appeared on earth while the elderly priest Zechariah burned incense and ministered in the temple. Gabriel came to tell Zechariah that his elderly wife,

Elizabeth, was going to conceive and bear a son. *Luke 1:19* records the event:

> *"And the angel answering said unto him, I am Gabriel, that stand in the presence of God; I am sent to speak unto thee, and to show thee these glad tidings."*

We read further in *Luke 1:26,27* that Gabriel was sent from God with a message to Mary as well. Again in *Luke 2:8,* the angel of the Lord appeared to the shepherds and announced the birth of Jesus. Although Scripture doesn't give the angel's name here, who could it have been but that same Gabriel, the one who had appeared to Zechariah and Mary with special messages from God! This was a special message, also, because the Bible says that "suddenly there was with the angel a multitude of the heavenly host praising God, and saying, Glory to God in the highest, and on earth peace, good will toward men."

Gabriel was given charge over the messenger angels. Who else could have led this song of celebration?

A second group of angels is the Warring Angels led by the archangel Michael. They are the soldiers of heaven, created by God to make war and keep the peace in that unseen world until the devil and all of his cohorts are consigned to hell and the door is shut forever.

The prophet Daniel had been fasting for 21 days when he wrote of Michael and the warring angels in *Daniel 10:2,3*:

> *"In those days I Daniel was mourning three full weeks. I ate no pleasant bread,*

*neither came flesh nor wine in my mouth,
neither did I anoint myself at all, till three
whole weeks were fulfilled."*

In verses 12 and 13 of the same chapter we read:

> *"Then said he unto me, Fear not,
> Daniel: for from the first day that thou
> didst set thine heart to understand, and
> to chasten thyself before thy God, thy
> words were heard, and I am come for thy
> words. But the prince of the kingdom of
> Persia withstood me one and twenty days:
> but, lo, Michael, one of the chief princes,
> came to help me; and I remained there
> with the kings of Persia."*

Why did Michael come to help this messenger angel
deliver his news to Daniel? First of all, the angel on that
important mission was created with the ability to deliver
God's news — not as a warrior. On this particular occa-
sion, the devil didn't want the message to get through
to God's servant so he hindered this messenger angel
until reinforcements were necessary.

The second reason, and the reason Michael himself
was sent to help the messenger angel, was because
Michael was the "Commander General" of the armies of
heaven. He knew how to fight: he had both strategy and
power. It is from this same group of angels that God
sends help today to His children to help them in their
everyday battles of life. Scripture confirms this in *Hebrews 1:13,14*:

3

> *"But to which of the angels said he at
> any time, Sit on my right hand, until I
> make thine enemies thy footstool? Are
> they not all ministering spirits, sent forth
> to minister for them who shall be heirs
> of salvation?"*

While God's Word clearly instructs us not to pray to angels, but only to God *(Matthew 6:9),* His angels are there to help us. They are God's agents to minister to our needs in a variety of ways. These heavenly agents help us learn who we are in Christ; they teach us what our rights and privileges are as Christians; they help us know the Word of God and its provisions for getting the help we need in times of trouble. Hear what the Word of God says in *Psalm 103:20:*

> *"Bless the Lord, ye his angels, that excel
> in strength, that do his commandments,
> hearkening unto the voice of his word."*

I have talked about the first two groups of angels to help you understand the third group: the Worship Angels. They were created to worship God. Lucifer had charge over these angels, but he was not an archangel. He was a cherub. In fact, he was called the "anointed cherub that covereth" and was the cherub of the cherubim. Isaiah wrote:

> *"Hell from beneath is moved for thee
> to meet thee at thy coming: it stirreth up
> the dead for thee, even all the chief ones
> of the earth; it hath raised up from their*

thrones all the kings of the nations.

"All they shall speak and say unto thee, Art thou also become weak as we? Art thou become like unto us? Thy pomp is brought down to the grave, and the noise of thy viols: the worm is spread under thee, and the worms cover thee.

"How art thou fallen from heaven, O Lucifer, son of the morning! How art thou cut down to the ground, which didst weaken the nations!

"For thou hast said in thine heart, I will ascend into heaven, I will exalt my throne above the stars of God: I will sit also upon the mount of the congregation, in the sides of the north: I will ascend above the heights of the clouds: I will be like the most High.

"Yet thou shalt be brought down to hell, to the sides of the pit."

(Isaiah 14:9-15)

Ezekiel commented:

"Thou hast been in Eden the garden of God; every precious stone was thy covering, the sardius, topaz, and the diamond,

the beryl, the onyx, and the jasper, the sapphire, the emerald, and the carbuncle, and gold: the workmanship of thy tabrets and of thy pipes was prepared in thee in the day that thou wast created.

"Thou art the anointed cherub that covereth; and I have set thee so: thou wast upon the holy mountain of God; thou hast walked up and down in the midst of the stones of fire. Thou wast perfect in thy ways from the day that thou wast created, till iniquity was found in thee.

"By the multitude of thy merchandise they have filled the midst of thee with violence, and thou hast sinned: therefore I will cast thee as profane out of the mountain of God: and I will destroy thee, O covering cherub, from the midst of the stones of fire.

"Thine heart was lifted up because of thy beauty, thou hast corrupted thy wisdom by reason of thy brightness: I will cast thee to the ground, I will lay thee before kings, that they may behold thee.

"Thou hast defiled thy sanctuaries by the multitude of thine iniquities, by the iniquity of thy traffick; therefore will I bring forth a fire from the midst of thee, it shall devour thee, and I will bring thee

*to ashes upon the earth in the sight of all
them that behold thee.*

*"All they that know thee among the
people shall be astonished at thee: thou
shalt be a terror, and never shalt thou be
any more."*

(Ezekiel 28:13-19)

So what does all that mean to you and me? In *Romans
1:20* Paul tells us we can understand the things we can't
see by learning from the things we can see. Jesus used
this method of storytelling to impart many truths to
people who couldn't otherwise grasp His message. He
told of a diligent housewife sweeping the house until
she found a lost coin — that emphasized how much care
He would put into the search for even one lost soul.
And of course the great parables of the sheep and their
shepherd have reached many a hardened, stiff heart.
Sometimes God instructed people to build things they
could see here on earth to represent things they couldn't
see in the spirit world around them. In *Exodus 25,* He
talked to Moses about building the Ark of the Covenant
to help Israel understand just how their God communi-
cated with them.

One major part of the Ark was the Mercy Seat, which
represented the throne of God in heaven. Over that
Mercy Seat stood two golden cherubim, which were
created heavenly beings. Lucifer was a cherubim — remember, that's what Ezekiel called him. The cherubim
covering the Mercy Seat represented Lucifer covering
the throne of God in heaven. No doubt he covered that
throne with praise and songs of worship, in the begin-

7

ning. God had created him for that purpose and set him in that place.

Lucifer was upon the holy mountain of God. How impossible it seems to us that he could have become so filled with pride and "lifted up" or boastful in himself. As my dad would have said, Lucifer "got too big for his britches that day." He sinned against God and tried to take the throne.

That day, there was war in heaven. Lucifer was stripped of all the power and authority he had with God. We read the words of Jesus in *Luke 10:18: "I beheld Satan as lightning fall from heaven."* What a terrible sight that must have been as God thrust His fallen creation out of heaven to be confined to the earth! God covered this earth with water, put a shroud of darkness around it, and marooned them in dark space.

Only God knows how many millions of years our planet hung in space in that condition. One day, He decided to straighten it out and put another created being here to rule it and bring it back to the Creator. We read about this in *Genesis 1:26 and 2:7:*

> *"And God said, Let us make man in our image, after our likeness: and let them have dominion over the fish of the sea, and over the fowl of the air, and over the cattle, and over all the earth, and over every creeping thing that creepeth upon the earth."*

> *"And the Lord God formed man of the dust of the ground, and breathed into his*

*nostrils the breath of life; and man be-
came a living soul."*

In the original Hebrew text, it says God "spirited" into man the spirit of life and man became a spirited soul; he was a soul with a spirit, an intellectual being yet capable of communing in spirit with his Creator. Man was body, soul, and spirit.

God gave this triune, threefold, being the power and authority that had been taken away from Lucifer. We find that the word "dominion" in *Genesis 1:26* is a word meaning "power and authority." Armed with this under-standing, we realize what Paul was talking about in *I Timothy 2:14,* that "Adam was not deceived." Of his own free will, knowing that what he was doing was forbidden, Adam handed all that power and authority back over to the devil. But why did he do it? Let's take a closer look.

Chapter 2
The responsibility of free will...

"I form the light, and create darkness:
I make peace, and create evil: I the Lord
do all these things." (Isaiah 45:7)

The first question most of us ask is, "How can a holy God create — or even <u>allow</u> — the existence of evil?" Why does He let such a monstrous force loose in the world?

There couldn't be an "up" without a "down." There couldn't be a "wide" if there wasn't a "narrow." There couldn't be "thick" without "thin." God created all of His created beings who were made <u>in His image</u>, the human race, with a free will. And in order that we might be able to <u>choose</u> His ways and His purpose, God had to allow the existence of evil alongside good. He never intended man to choose evil, but He had to allow its existence and allow man the choice. Or it would have been "no contest."

When Lucifer decided to step out of God's realm of good and into his own realm of evil, God allowed him to do so. He did not force His will on the disobedient cherub. However, Lucifer's behavior brought its own repercussions. It was the first recorded occurrence of sin in the universe and this destructive, self-seeking behavior brought separation from God. (See Chart #2)

In the Garden of Eden, Adam did the same thing. Until Adam sinned, he walked and lived and was ruled by his spirit man. He chose that which was edifying and creative and of God. But when of his own free will Adam stepped out of the realm of good into the realm of evil, his spirit man died and carnal man took over the rulership of his life. Instead of the spirit of eternal life pulsing through his veins, death began to work. Ever since then, the human race has been plagued with carnality and death.

Paul wrote about this in *I Corinthians 3:1-4*, where we read:

> *"And I, brethren, could not speak unto you as unto spiritual, but as unto carnal, even as unto babes in Christ. I have fed you with milk, and not with meat: for hitherto ye were not able to bear it, neither yet now are ye able.*
>
> *"For ye are yet carnal: for whereas there is among you envying, and strife, and divisions, are ye not carnal, and walk as men? For while one saith, I am of Paul, and another, I am of Apollos; are ye not carnal?"*

The carnal man will not be brought into subjection

11

except as we put him to death. With Paul, we have to say, "I die daily" — meaning we put to death and keep a constant guard on the desires and appetites of our flesh. In the Amplified Bible *Romans 5:12,14* tells us:

> *"Wherefore as sin came into the world through one man and death as the result of sin, so death spread to all men, (no one being able to stop it or to escape its power) because all men sinned.*
>
> *"Yet death held sway from Adam to Moses (the Lawgiver), even over those who did not themselves transgress (a positive command) as Adam did. Adam was a type (prefigure) of the One Who was to come (but in reverse; the former destructive, the latter saving).*

Why did death hold sway from Adam to Moses? Simply because during that time there was no visible hope for deliverance from death; but with the appearance of Moses on the scene there came a glimmer of hope. Moses was another early type, or symbol, of things to come. He represented the Christ who would defeat death. He led Israel out of bondage toward the Promised Land. Jesus himself remarked about Moses' foreshadowing of events to come when he said, *"And as Moses lifted up the serpent in the wilderness, even so must the Son of man be lifted up"* (John 3:14).

Moses' mission as a forerunner of Christ is detailed in *Deuteronomy 18:18,* quoted here from the Amplified Bible:

12

"I will raise up for them a prophet from among their brethren, like you, and will put My words in his mouth; and he shall speak to them all that I command him."

Paul says in *II Corinthians 1:9* that before Christ:

"We had the sentence of death in ourselves, that we should not trust in ourselves, but in God which raiseth the dead: Who delivered us from so great a death, and doth deliver: in whom we trust that he will yet deliver."

And in *Hebrews 2:14,15* we read:

"Forasmuch then as the children are partakers of flesh and blood, he also himself likewise took part of the same; that through death he might destroy him that had the power of death, that is, the devil; And deliver them who through fear of death were all their lifetime subject to bondage."

Christ took upon himself human flesh so that, as a human being, yet fully and powerfully God, He could destroy the devil who had brought the pain of death to earth and deliver us up from both physical and spiritual death.

Now there is real hope. When we walk in the Spirit, and let our spirit man be in the driver's seat of our life, we do not have to fear death any more. Of course, the carnal and natural man won't meekly take a back seat. The struggle will always be there.

In *Romans 7:14-23* Paul writes about the struggle he has between the carnal (fleshly) man and the spirit man:

"We know that the Law is spiritual; but I am a creature of the flesh (carnal, unspiritual), having been sold into slavery under (the control of) sin.

"For I do not understand my own actions — I am baffled, bewildered. I do not practice or accomplish what I wish, but I do the very thing that I loathe (which my moral instinct condemns). Now if I do (habitually) what is contrary to my desire, (that means that) I acknowledge and agree that the Law is good (morally excellent) and that I take sides with it.

"However, it is no longer I who do the deed, but the sin (principle) which is at home in me and has possession of me.

"For I know that nothing good dwells within me, that is, in my flesh. I can will what is right, but I cannot perform it. I have the intention and urge to do what is right, but no power to carry it out;

"For I fail to practice the good deeds I desire to do, but the evil deeds that I do

not desire to do are what I am (ever) doing. Now if I do what I do not desire to do, it is no longer I doing it — it is not myself that acts — but the sin (principle) which dwells within me (fixed and operating in my soul).

"So I find it to be a law (of my being) that when I want to do what is right and good, evil is ever present with me and I am subject to its insistent demands. For I endorse and delight in the Law of God in my inmost self — with my new nature. But I discern in my bodily members — in the sensitive appetites and wills of the flesh — a different law (rule of action) at war against the law of my mind (my reason) and making me a prisoner to the law of sin that dwells in my bodily organs — in the sensitive appetites and wills of the flesh."

Notice in verse 17 Paul says *"it is no longer I who do the deed, but the sin principle which is at home in me, and has possession of me."* And in verse 20 he writes, *"If I do what I don't desire to do, it is not myself acting, but the sin principle which is fixed and operating in my soul."* He says that the sin principle, which is the ability to sin, is <u>fixed and operating in his soul</u>.

When Adam disobeyed God, his spirit man died. His soulish man and his carnal man teamed up to rule his life. The carnal man had the upper hand, with the sin principle fixed and operating in Adam's soul. Through the door of Adam's sin, this evil walks close by all of us.

What did God say to Cain in *Genesis 4:6,7?* He said, *"Why art thou wroth? and why is thy countenance fallen? If thou doest well, shalt thou not be accepted? and if thou doest not well, sin lieth at the door."* It makes no difference how saved we are, sin isn't very far away from any of us! The sin principle, or the ability to sin, is with us as long as we live in this world.

Sin is like a rattlesnake under a bush, ready to strike at the first opportunity. Paul warns in *Romans 8:5,7:*

> *"For those who are according to the flesh and controlled by its unholy desires set their minds on and pursue those things which gratify the flesh. But those who are according to the Spirit and (controlled by the desires) of the Spirit, set their minds on and seek those things which gratify the (Holy) Spirit.*
>
> *"(That is) Because the mind of the flesh — with its carnal thoughts and purposes — is hostile to God; for it does not submit itself to God's law; indeed, it cannot."*

We need to keep on our guard, stay prayed up and in touch with God — or the carnal man will rule our life.

Is it possible to be a carnal Christian?

My understanding from Scripture is this: It is possible for a time, but not for very long. Let me pause right here and say I do not believe anyone <u>should</u> be a carnal Christian. I think every Christian should live as close to Christ and as far away from sin as possible. However, I want to put this in balance.

It has been my observation as a pastor, evangelist, missionary, and teacher for over 30 years that new Christians often get discouraged because when they come out of Egypt, all of Egypt does not come out of them at the same time. Perhaps I can explain this more fully...with Moses' story.

Do you remember when the day finally came that Israel was led out of Egypt after the death angel visited the Egyptians' homes and passed over the homes of the Israelites, who had sprinkled their doorposts with the blood of a sacrificial offering? They were no sooner across the Red Sea than many of them began to long for the "leeks and garlic" of Egypt. They were glad to be free from Egyptian bondage...but they couldn't quite let go of <u>all</u> they had known during their years of slavery.

Sometimes new Christians still have habits and other things they want to hang onto...or that want to hang onto them. Then some well-meaning Christian brother or sister who has been "in the way" — figuratively and literally — who should know better, may point an accusing finger at those habits or leftovers from the old life and begin to criticize and condemn. The new Christian finds himself at the end of a loaded gun rather than under a protective wing, many times.

He may become discouraged and give up because he is condemned for the scraps of carnality he hasn't yet shed. Rather than condemnation, he needs encouragement. He needs to hear someone say, "I had some awful problems when I first became a Christian. I had some

17

habits I couldn't let go of right away — or that wouldn't let go of me. But you know, I kept working at it, and the brothers and sisters in my church family prayed for me and with me, and before long those leftovers from my old life began to melt away. Not all at once, and not as fast as they might have, but now by the grace of God I'm free of most of them. I'm still working on a few myself."

Do you see the difference? The new Christian needs to be encouraged by pointing him to an important truth of Christian living recorded in *II Peter 3:18, "But grow in grace, and in the knowledge of our Lord and Saviour Jesus Christ."*

Salvation is a cleaning, a washing-away, of our sins. It is instant. It happens in a second when God sees us for the first time through the blood of His Son, a new, cleansed creation.

Living the Christian life, on the other hand, is a growth process. Just as a child outgrows one phase of life, or one size of clothes, and grows into another, so we as Christians outgrow some ideas and behaviors that are less Christlike and grow into others that are more Christlike. We grow in grace, and in the knowledge of our Lord and Saviour Jesus Christ. That part of our new life isn't instant. It's planted, cultivated, and slowly harvested.

When our daughter was betwen the ages of 10 and 12, it seemed we could buy her a dress in town and she would be too tall for it before we got home. But while she was outgrowing that one, she was growing into another one.

When our son was two or three years old, he would lay back in my arms and pretend to be a little baby and say, "I'm your ga-ga baby." It was cute then, and I loved

18

to play the game with him. But today he's 25 years old, stands 6' tall, and weighs 210 pounds. He lifts weights, has a good job, and a lovely wife. If he came up to me today and wanted me to pick him up so he could lay back in my arms and say "I'm your ga-ga baby," it wouldn't be so funny. I'd know he was severely disturbed and in need of professional help.

Most of us had cute, childish habits that we had to grow out of as we matured because they weren't so desirable any longer. And most of us as Christians have habits and ways that we need to grow out of as our understanding of God's Word and His love for us deepens.

This is part of the lesson God began to teach me years ago in the Louisiana piney woods as I walked and prayed and cried and sought His presence. The sooner we can learn how to grow out of our self-defeating, self-condemning ways, and quit looking at our failures and shortcomings, the better off we will be.

> *We come into God's kingdom with a lot*
> *of excess baggage. And we have to learn*
> *what to keep and what to leave behind.*

New Christians who are still a little bit "carnal" don't hinder the work of the church nearly as much as people who have been "in the way" while they were "on the way" for 30-40 years. I don't mind giving the bottle Paul talked about to that spiritual baby, but I sure do hate to have to part the whiskers to get the nipple in his mouth! After 30-40 years, it's long past time to put the bottle away and save it for the next baby.

In *I Corinthians 3:1-4,* Paul says four times that the

Corinthian Christians are carnal; yet, in *I Corinthians 1:11, 2:1, and 3:1,* he calls those same people "brethren." Paul reserves that description for believers. These carnal people have experienced salvation; they are "on the way" to heaven, but they still have a lot of baggage from yesterday that's "in the way." And they need to lighten their load.

In *Matthew 13:3-23* Jesus gives the parable of the sower — again, to help us understand what we can't see by explaining it in terms we can "see."

> *"And he spake many things unto them in parables, saying, Behold, a sower went forth to sow; And when he sowed, some seeds fell by the way side, and the fowls came and devoured them up:*
>
> *"Some fell upon stony places, where they had not much earth: and forthwith they sprung up, because they had no deepness of earth: And when the sun was up, they were scorched; and because they had no root, they withered away.*
>
> *"And some fell among thorns; and the thorns sprung up, and choked them:*
>
> *"But others fell into good ground, and brought forth fruit, some an hundredfold, some sixtyfold, and some thirtyfold."*

In these verses, Jesus plainly shows the effect the gospel has on each part of the human being. Notice first that the sower sowed the seed <u>without discrimination</u>. That's the way God does. He doesn't look at one person and say, "The effect of my Word will go no deeper than the flesh."

Neither does He look at another person and say, "The Word will go no deeper than the natural man, so I won't sow the gospel there."

God sees to it that the seed of the gospel is sown to every man the same. But it is up to the individual how far that seed penetrates his life. Let's look at the rest of the parable from *Matthew 13:*

> *"But he that received the seed into stony places, the same is he that heareth the word, and anon with joy receiveth it; Yet hath he not root in himself, but dureth for a while: for when tribulation or persecution ariseth because of the word, by and by he is offended.*
>
> *"He also that received seed among the thorns is he that heareth the word; and the cares of this world, and the deceitfulness of riches, choke the word, and he becometh unfruitful."*

The effect of the gospel in this person's life went no deeper than the fleshly, carnal man. The seed of the gospel was received with joy and sprang up quickly. It felt good to the flesh and had an effect for a time, but it didn't last.

Jesus said in verse 21 that this person had no root in himself. Nothing of value will grow in rocky soil, even

21

though the very best seed might have been planted there. *Matthew 13:19* says, *"When anyone heareth the word and <u>understandeth it not</u>, then cometh the wicked one, and catcheth away that which was sown in his heart."* This is the natural man, the natural mind. This part of a man's being cannot understand the things of God. In *I Corinthians 2:14* we read,

> *"The natural man receiveth not the things of the spirit of God: for they are foolishness unto him: neither can he know them, because they are spiritually discerned." Or, we might say they are only understood by the spirit man. The part which seeks to bring man back into oneness with God.*

Now let's look at *Matthew 13:23*:

> *"But he that received seed into the good ground is he that heareth the word, and understandeth it; which also beareth fruit, and bringeth forth, some an hundredfold, some sixty, and some thirty."*

Here the effect of the gospel goes deeper than the flesh; deeper than the natural mind. It goes down into the spirit of the individual and finds good soil, "heart soil," takes root, and produces fruit. This is what finally happened to Paul. But it didn't happen right away, even to this apostle who had such a dramatic encounter with Christ.

In *II Corinthians 5:16,* Paul says there was a time in his life when he knew Christ only after the flesh; but he also said, "I don't know Him that way any more." We read in *Philippians 3:3-8:*

> *"For we are the circumcision, which worship God in the spirit, rejoice in Christ Jesus, and have no confidence in the flesh. Though I might also have confidence in the flesh. If any other man thinketh that he hath whereof he might trust in the flesh, I more:*

> *"Circumcised the eighth day, of the stock of Israel, of the tribe of Benjamin, an Hebrew of the Hebrews; as touching the law, a Pharisee; Concerning zeal, persecuting the church; touching the righteousness which is in the law, blameless.*

> *"But what things were gain to me, those I counted loss for Christ. Yea doubtless, and I count all things but loss for the excellency of the knowledge of Christ Jesus my Lord: for whom I have suffered the loss of all things, and do count them but dung, that I may win Christ."*

Paul was a "Jew's Jew"...and if anyone ever had a reason to have confidence in the power of the flesh to get him through this life and safely into the next one, it was Paul: he was circumcised the eighth day after birth as was the Jewish custom; he was of the stock of Israel, of the tribe of Benjamin, so his credentials were good; he was a Hebrew of the Hebrews; he knew the Mosaic law inside-out; he was a zealous persecutor of the infant Christian church before his conversion; and he not only <u>knew</u> the law but he <u>kept</u> the law as it related to righteousness before God.

Yet, Paul realized and publicly said that everything he was, everything he had, even his flesh, he counted as nothing but barnyard fertilizer because he knew, finally, what was the better way. He shared that secret in *Philippians 3:9,10:*

> *"And be found in him, not having mine own righteousness, which is of the law, but that which is through the faith of Christ, the righteousness which is of God by faith;*
>
> *"That I may know him, and the power of his resurrection, and the fellowship of his sufferings, being made conformable unto his death."*

"That I may know him, and his power...and his sufferings if need be...and be made conformable to His death...the death that gave life." That's what Paul discovered to be the secret of confidence. It was the confidence of putting the spirit man in control and allowing the Holy Spirit to direct his life into a closer image of Christ's life.

Chapter 3
"Y' are so!" "Am not!" "Are so!"

We used to sing an old song about how topsy turvy things often get in the church — it went like this: "It's not the preacher, nor the deacon, but it's me, O Lord, standin' in the need of prayer!" I think that's what Paul was feeling when he wrote to the church at Corinth, in *I Corinthians 1:10-13:*

> *"Now I beseech you, brethren, by the name of our Lord Jesus Christ, that ye all speak the same thing, and that there be no divisions among you; but that ye be perfectly joined together in the same mind and in the same judgment.*

> *"For it hath been declared unto me of you, my brethren, by them which are of the house of Chloe, that there are contentions among you.*

> *"Now this I say, that every one of you saith, I am of Paul; and I of Apollos; and I of Cephas; and I of Christ.*
>
> *"Is Christ divided? was Paul crucified for you? or were ye baptized in the name of Paul?*

Verse 12 explains why there were factions in the Corinthian church. One group said they were of Paul, another group said they were of Apollos. Still another said they were of Cephas. But one group had their thinking straight; they said they were of Christ!

In verse 13, Paul asked this entire church the key question, and we'll come back to it again, but think with me about what he said.

> *"Is Christ divided?"*

As I see it, there were two reasons why the church at Corinth had problems: 1) They were still carnal to varying degrees, and 2) They were trying to do something about it and grow up spiritually.

If you are a carnal Christian and content to remain so, it seems you don't have too many spiritual problems. You won't run head-on into the devil if you're both going the same way. But if you as an individual or the church as a body start trying to grow up in Christ, the devil starts fighting and opposing you. You'll meet him at every turn, for he knows that if the church ever gets filled with adult, mature, stable, established Christians, he'll have more trouble on his back than he can slither away from.

Consequently, the devil tries to keep the Christians

as carnal as he can, coaxing them back away from their first halting steps toward God into a life of "just a little" sin — whatever that is. If he can't succeed in that, he starts trying to divide them in the church by causing strife and fighting. Picture what he must have accomplished in Corinth alone...

Apollos, with his group, always sat on the left side of the building. They wanted to buy a new piano and fix the holes in the church roof. Cephas sat with his group on the right side of the building. He wanted to repave the parking lot and maybe buy a little stained-glass window to put in the back of the building above the pulpit. Paul's group sat in the back and grumbled because they wanted to buy the preacher a set of new tires for his car and maybe hire an assistant to help run the church. And there wasn't enough money in the treasury for all three groups to have what they wanted. So their initial arguments got hotter, and took in wider subjects, until the church was divided and about to smell pretty rotten!

Let me pause here for just a moment to say that you won't ever find a perfect church — and if you should find one, don't join it. There's something wrong somewhere. Count on that. Take it all the way to the bank.

But God's people, and His churches, don't have to be that way. We don't have to be ignorant of Satan's devices. In *II Corinthians 2:11* Paul says, *"Lest Satan should get an advantage of us, for we are not ignorant of his devices."* Yet so many of God's people are ignorant of the devil's tricks and the fact that there are only two Scriptural reasons why God's people perish spiritually:

1) "My people are destroyed for lack of knowledge" (Hosea 4:6)

*2) "Where there is no vision, the people
perish" (Proverbs 29:18)*

What kind of knowledge was Hosea talking about? A
knowledge of the world? No. <u>We perish from our lack
of knowledge of God's Word!</u> The devil doesn't care
how many Bibles you have as long as they are safe on
the closet shelf covered with dust. But if you ever start
to <u>read</u> one of those Bibles, you are going to gain knowledge — not only of God, but of the devil and his tricks,
also. And this is exactly what Satan doesn't want.

In order to win the battle, and eventually the war, you
have to know your enemy. That is why the United States
was able to win World Wars I and II. Our commanders
knew their enemy; they knew his battle plans; they broke
his secret code messages; they learned to spot his
camouflaged troops.

One of the devil's greatest assets in causing division
in the church is his camouflage. How often he even hides
behind something as innocent and potentially produc-
tive as a church business meeting! He stirs a little here,
adds a little of his own special "hot sauce" there, creates
a big argument, and cackles as the church splits because
the people can't see him in the bitter attacks they hurl
at each other.

The Bible warns us about his attacks in the church,
in *Galatians 5:13-15* (quoting from The Amplified
Bible):

> *"For you, brethren, were (indeed)
> called to freedom; only (do not let your)
> freedom be an incentive to your flesh and
> an opportunity or excuse (for selfish-*

ness), but through love you should serve one another.

"For the whole Law (concerning human relationships) is complied with in the one precept, You shall love your neighbor as yourself.

"But if you bite and devour one another (in partisan strife), be careful that you (and your whole fellowship) are not consumed by one another."

Let's look again at verse 15: *"But if you bite and devour one another in partisan strife (or party spirit), be careful that you and your whole fellowship are not consumed by one another."* If the devil can get the church fighting within itself, that is better than a direct attack they can identify from outside the church. They may not even know what hit them! But to do that, he has to keep God's people ignorant of his tricks.

Let's take just a short look at the second reason God's people perish spiritually, *"Where there is no vision, the people perish" (Proverbs 29:18).* The kind of vision referred to here is spiritual vision. Keeping our spiritual eyes on our spiritual model; with our spiritual heritage and power in control; in other words, putting the spirit man in total command. If we don't make this persistent effort to put the spirit man in command of our daily lives, we will perish. Spiritually perish. We don't need to fear physical death — because Paul said that to be absent from the body is to be present with the Lord.

That's nothing to fear. But what we need to guard against is the kind of spiritual death Proverbs warns us about. Over and over again, God's Word uses the metaphor of blindness in the physical life to teach about spiritual blindness. This kind of sightlessness brings spiritual death. And Satan offers it in a variety of settings that seem, at first glance, appealing. The wine is "red in the cup," as Proverbs reminds us in another verse.

Let's go to *Genesis 3:8-13* for another look:

> *"And they heard the voice of the Lord God walking in the garden in the cool of the day: and Adam and his wife hid themselves from the presence of the Lord God amongst the trees of the garden.*

> *"And the Lord God called unto Adam, and said unto him, Where art thou?*

> *"And he said, I heard thy voice in the garden, and I was afraid, because I was naked; and I hid myself.*

> *"And he said, "Who told thee that thou wast naked? Hast thou eaten of the tree, whereof I commanded thee that thou shouldest not eat?*

> *"And the man said, The woman whom thou gavest to be with me, she gave me of the tree, and I did eat.*

> *"And the Lord God said unto the*

woman, What is this that thou hast done? And the woman said, The serpent beguiled me, and I did eat."

When God came into the garden to have fellowship with Adam and Eve, they had hidden themselves because they had disobeyed and through the knowledge they gained in that act, they discovered they were naked. Then they felt guilty — for eating the fruit, or being naked, or both — and they hid. When God asked Adam if he had eaten of the tree, he blamed it on the woman. Contention between a man and wife showed its ugly face for the first time, and Eve decided to protect herself. In verse 13, when God asked her what she had done, she blamed it on the serpent.

The carnal man was in the driver's seat of human lives for the first time. Adam accused Eve. Eve accused the devil. Can you hear them? "You did so." "I did not." "Yes you did. I saw you." "Prove it!"

Contrast this with *Job 1:22* where this godly man suffered the loss of all his possessions and even the lives of his children, yet the Scripture gives this witness of Job's faith and the spirit man who controlled his life: *"In all this Job sinned not, nor charged God foolishly."*

Again, in *Job 2:9,10* we read:

"Then said his wife unto him, Dost thou still retain thine integrity? curse God, and die.

"But he said unto her, Thou speakest as one of the foolish women speaketh.

> *What? shall we receive good at the hand*
> *of God, and shall we not receive evil? In*
> *all this did not Job sin with his lips."*

I can just hear Mrs. Job wailing, "Well, you've blessed God all your life, and now look at how God is treating you. Why don't you just curse God and die? Go ahead. I dare you."

And I can hear the spirit man in Job answering levelly, "Woman, don't be a fool. God has given me the good things I've had in life. He may have allowed the bad things to exist, but He didn't cause them to happen. We can't expect just good in life. Woman, there can't be an 'up' without a 'down.' This is the 'down.' Just be patient. This will pass. You'll see."

Job was able to maintain his integrity and refuse to accuse God of causing his troubles because the spirit man was in control of his life. Hallelujah! What a contrast between Job and Adam!

"See you in ~~church~~ court...

Turn now to *I Corinthians 6:18,* and we'll read together about another device the enemy uses to drive his splitting wedge deeper into the heart of the church:

> *"Dare any of you, having a matter*
> *against another, go to law before the un-*
> *just, and not before the saints?*

> *"Do ye not know that the saints shall*

*judge the world? and if the world shall
be judged by you, are ye unworthy to
judge the smallest matters?*

*"Know ye not that we shall judge
angels? how much more things that per-
tain to this life?*

*"If then ye have judgments of things
pertaining to this life, set them to judge
who are least esteemed in the church.*

*"I speak to your shame. Is it so, that
there is not a wise man among you? No,
not one that shall be able to judge between his brethren?*

*"But brother goeth to law with brother,
and that before the unbelievers.*

*"Now therefore there is utterly a fault
among you, because ye go to law one
with another. Why do ye not rather take
wrong? Why do ye not rather suffer yourselves to be defrauded?*

*"Nay, ye do wrong, and defraud, and
that your brethren."*

We're back now to another of Satan's favorite tactics
— if he can't get us to accuse God for our troubles, he'll
keep working away at dividing the Body of Christ. Either
way, carnal man is in control when this happens. If he

can't get us to accuse God, he's about as happy to have us picking at one another. Either way, we're not growing and the church is not growing. His barns are fat. God's are empty.

In this passage we've just looked at, Paul rebukes Christians for going to law before unsaved, unjust judges. Some have taken this to mean that a Christian should never go to court for any reason. That is not the meaning of this scripture. If someone runs into you with a car, and it is his fault and he won't make it right according to law, then you have every right to take your case to court for the settlement of just damages.

The Christians at Corinth were hauling one another into court over spirit<u>spiritual</u> matters! Someone would begin to prophecy or give a message in other tongues* (*if this is new to you, you can read about it in *Acts Chapters 1 and 2),* and someone else would stand up and begin to do the same thing. The first person would take his brother to a Roman court, before an unsaved judge, and bring suit because his own message was interrupted. They accused one another because they were carnal.

Paul rebuked them for this. In *I Corinthians 6:7,8* he asked them why they didn't just accept the wrong their brother had done, say nothing, or at least say something but say it privately, instead of doing wrong to their brother and bringing embarrassment upon the church by going to a Roman court of law. It is such a sad thing to see Christians accusing one another. One of the most destructive things is to see a Christian mom and dad accusing one another, often in front of the children, and then put on a smile and go to church without ever resolving their problems or getting things right between the two of them. Then they wonder why they can't get

34

their children inside a church after they're grown and gone from home. These children have seen such a double standard all their lives that they have no confidence in their parents or the apparently useless faith their parents have preached to them for so many years. Isn't it amazing how two lives, joined together in love, pledging to love and cherish each other forever, can be torn apart by a finger pointed in hateful accusation and a willing mouth to back it up!

In this instance of the family and in *I Corinthians 6:1-8* where brother is taking brother to court, Satan is using the carnal man to divide and weaken the Body of Christ. Make no mistake: Satan freely uses Christians who are ignorant of his devices! He'll find them anyplace in the Body of Christ they exist. One of the greatest revelations God ever gave me from His Word on this subject — or any other — is from *Matthew 16:13-23.*

Jesus had asked His disciples a question: *"Whom do men say that I, the son of man, am?"* Some answered one thing, some another, but Simon Peter spoke up with the answer: *"Thou art the Christ, the Son of the living God."* Jesus got so excited, and pronounced a long blessing on him! In verse 17 Jesus said, *"Blessed art thou, Simon Barjona: for flesh and blood hath not revealed it unto thee, but my Father which is in heaven."*

Then in verse 21, Jesus began to talk about His coming death and the things he would have to suffer at the hands of the elders, the chief priests, and the scribes. Peter rebuked the Lord for saying what He did. Maybe Peter was frightened. Maybe he was trying to smooth over what they all knew was coming very soon. But in any event, in verse 23 we read:

35

> *"But he (Jesus) turned, and said unto Peter, Get thee behind me, Satan: thou art an offence unto me: for thou savourest not the things that be of God, but those that be of men."*

In one breath, God was speaking through Peter. In the next breath, the devil was putting ideas in Peter's head and speaking through him. How could this be? In the first instance, the spirit man was in control. In the second, the carnal man had taken over the driver's seat. It's the same lament that Paul wrote about in *Romans Chapter 7.* There is that constant battle to do good — to put the spirit man in control — even as the enemy sneaks in to drive a sliver of rebellion in here...a wedge of bitterness there...a root of unresolved family trouble just a little farther down the pew...

As we have seen in *I Corinthians 6:1-8,* the devil used the carnal man in an attempt to divide and wreck the church. Why? Because he saw the church beginning to grow up. They were growing out of some of the excess baggage we talked about earlier. Paul had reminded them, as recorded in *I Corinthians 6:9,10,* who would not inherit the Kingdom of God; some specific kinds of baggage they'd have to unload if they wanted to experience this inheritance: the unrighteous, the fornicators, idolators, adulterers, homesexuals, thieves, the covetous, drunkards, revilers, and extortioners.

He says, in verse 11, *"And such were some of you: but ye are washed, but ye are sanctified, but ye are justified in the name of the Lord Jesus, and by the spirit of our God."* In other words, he reminds them that although they used to live according to the flesh, it is now

36

time for them to grow up even farther and put the ways of the flesh farther behind them.

You may be thinking, Could the Corinthian Christians be this carnal? Did the church really have this kind of problem so close to the very time of Christ? Yes. They did. In *I Corinthians 11:1-16* we read about problems over a man cutting his hair and a woman not cutting hers; over a woman wearing a covering on her head when she came to church and a man not wearing anything on his head. Paul settled that problem in verse 16 when he informed them what the doctrine was really about...a woman with long, beautiful hair might draw more attention to herself than to her prophecy when she spoke out in church, so it was better for her to keep her head covered. Then the people would concentrate on the prophecy rather than the prophetess. If a man had long hair or short it made no difference in style — it probably meant he just hadn't gotten around to cutting it.

Paul even had to have a "Dutch Uncle" talk with them about the way they took communion in the Corinthian church. Let's look at his conversation with them in *I Corinthians 11:17-22:*

"Now in this that I declare unto you I praise you not, that ye come together not for the better, but for the worse.

"For first of all, when ye come together in the church, I hear that there be divisions among you; and I partly believe it.

"For there must be also heresies among

> *you, that they which are approved may be made manifest among you.*
>
> *When ye come together therefore into one place, this is not to eat the Lord's supper. For in eating every one taketh before other his own supper: and one is hungry, and another is drunken.*
>
> *"What? have ye not houses to eat and to drink in? or despise ye the church of God, and shame them that have not? What shall I say to you? shall I praise you in this? I praise you not."*

Notice in verses 17 and 18 he says they don't come together for the betterment of each other, but for the worse. For, first of all, when they come together, there are divisions among them. He rebukes them further because the rich are bringing their sumptuous meals to the church and stuffing themselves while the poor watch from the other side of the room and go away as hungry as when they came. The rich are even getting drunk in the church!

Yet, while all of this is going on, the gifts of the Holy Spirit are in operation in the church. For, in the very next chapter, *I Corinthians 12,* Paul has to talk to them about their abuse and misuse of the gifts and instruct them on the gifts' operation and regulation. Perhaps this was yet another example of some new Christians who hadn't yet learned how to leave all of Egypt in Egypt...but Satan used it to wedge hurt and misunderstanding between people in the young church. Carnal man, you see,

see, doesn't drive by the rules. As daddy would have phrased it, he takes his half out in the middle of the road. Whatever's left over is for everybody else.

I remember many years ago, when some deacons and others in the hierarchy of the church, people I trusted, did me a grave injustice. They crushed me and hurt my family. I remember how my carnal man wanted to get even for that hurt. Especially for the hurt I felt it had caused my family. I fought with it for three long years. I could almost feel myself slipping back into that confused boy in the Louisiana piney woods walking and crying out to God, "I don't deserve this. I can't handle it. It's just not fair."

One day a dear friend of mine, missionary Morris Plotts, stopped by unexpectedly to see me. I shared with him what I was going through at the time. When I finished my story, he gave me the greatest advice I have ever been given. He said, "Charles, take the low road and God will exalt you."

I went on my knees later that day, beside my couch, lifted my hands to heaven, and began to pray. I had so much to empty out before anything good could come of this experience. I spoke the names of those who had hurt me and told God exactly how my fleshly person felt about them. And I didn't stop there. I told God how I had tried to love and forgive them, but I couldn't seem to do it.

"God," I prayed, "All I can do is open up my heart to you. Take away the hurt. Take away the bad feelings. Replace them with new ones. Love those people through me."

When I said that, it was like the flood gates of heaven were opened and the love of God poured through me, washing out all the hate, bitterness, and resentment. Praise God! The love of God will clean you out better than a roto-rooter!

This kind of "praying through," as the old-timers called it, can take a lot out of you in more ways than one. It's one of those times you really need to be alone with God in your prayer closet as you bring out for His eyes and ears alone the things you couldn't say to anyone else. When you do this kind of self-examination, which is what I believe Paul was talking about in *II Corinthians 13:5* you empty out the destructiveness of the carnal man's influence in your life and make plenty of room for God's spirit to poke His sunshine into the remotest corners until you've got a double load! It'll feel so good — you won't have to tell people who's in control of your life. They'll know to look at you that something good has happened!

As Paul closes his second letter to the Corinthian church, he answers the question he asks earlier in the chapter: *Is Christ divided?* In verse 11 of the last chapter of *II Corinthians* Paul reminds us that we must be of one mind — be like-minded as brothers and sisters in Christ. He is not — and cannot be — divided. Nor can we, if we would be His followers.

> *"Finally, brethren, rejoice, be made complete, be comforted, be like minded, live in peace; and the God of love and peace shall be with you. (II Corinthians 13:11, The Living Bible)*

One way the devil keeps the carnal man ignorant of the real source of his problems, like he did with Adam, is to encourage him to accuse others for his actions. He'll try to make man accuse God of causing his problems. Carnal man is so very reluctant to accept the responsibility for his sins and failures.

The natural man, whom we haven't talked much about yet, questions everything and always asks, "Why?" He tries to reason everything out. For some things, there are no logical reasons the natural, soulish man can find. The spirit man, finally, accepts whatever he is passing through as God's will for that particular time in his life and looks for what he can learn from it that will be of benefit to God's kingdom and His work on earth. He trusts God and praises Him anyhow.

By looking at the reaction of the carnal man, the natural man, and the spirit man, to what is happening in your life, you can tell who is in control and in the driver's seat. Is it the carnal man, accusing someone else of being responsible for the problems? Is it the natural man, always trying to figure out and reason out just what's happening? Is it the spirit man, trusting in God even though the circumstances may be beyond control and even beyond understanding?

As we come into fellowship with God and are babes in Christ, we'll most often find ourselves passing through a combination of these three "drivers" on the way through life's hard places. We learn, through experience and finding that we can always trust God's wisdom and care, to get quickly past the accusations of the carnal man, the questioning of the natural man, to the comfort of the spirit man who says "Praise God Anyhow!"

Chapter 4
Git while the gittin' 's good!

There have been some times in my life when I've seen folks who were "fleeing temptation" in the strangest way...it looked to me like they were crawling backwards on their hands and knees hoping it might catch up to them if they went slow enough. But that's not the kind of "fleeing" that we're going to study right now.

In this chapter we're going to take a look at the exposed tempter and some of his methods, and then explore some ways to leave him sittin' in the dust! First of all, then, let's get on solid Scriptural ground:

> *"Love not the world, neither the things that are in the world. If any man love the world, the love of the Father is not in him. For all that is in the world, the lust of the flesh, and the lust of the eyes, and the pride of life, is not of the Father, but is of the world. And the world passeth away,*

and the lust thereof, but he that doeth the will of God abideth forever" (1 John 2:15-17).

"Now the serpent was more subtle than any beast of the field which the Lord God had made. And he said unto the woman, Yea, hath God said, Ye shall not eat of every tree of the garden? And the woman said unto the serpent, We may eat of the fruit of the trees of the garden: But of the fruit of the tree which is in the midst of the garden, God hath said, Ye shall not eat of it, neither shall ye touch it, lest ye die.

"And the serpent said unto the woman, Ye shall not surely die: For God doth know that in the day ye eat thereof, then your eyes shall be opened, and ye shall be as gods, knowing good and evil.

"And when the woman saw that the tree was good for food, and that it was pleasant to the eyes, and a tree to be desired to make one wise, she took of the fruit thereof, and did eat, and gave also unto her husband with her; and he did eat.

"And the eyes of them both were opened, and they knew that they were naked; and they sewed fig leaves together, and made themselves aprons" (Genesis 3:1-7).

43

That very first temptation took place in the same three areas of the carnal man that John later warned Christians about: the lust of the flesh, the lust of the eyes, and the pride of life.

Genesis 3:6 describes Eve's lust of the flesh: *"...the woman saw that the tree was good for food,"* It also describes her lust of the eyes: *"...and that it was pleasant to the eyes."* This same verse also describes the pride of life as it was exhibited in Eve *"...a tree to be desired to make one wise."* Eve was tempted in all three areas at once! The devil wants us to think he can come against us from a thousand different directions at once, but the truth is, his power is limited. He can't do that. However, if he can keep us confused and believing that he can come from many different directions, he can keep us defeated.

Every temptation that comes against you and me comes from one or more of these three categories: the lust of the flesh, the lust of the eyes, and the pride of life. The devil cannot come against you any other way. When you realize this, you have narrowed his tricks and temptations down to where you can recognize them and use your God-given power to defeat his best attack.

We see from the third chapter of Genesis that even in a sinless state, because man was created a free moral agent with the ability to choose between good and evil, the infant carnal man had his fleshly appetites already fully developed and could be tempted.

Before you get too upset about that, remember what we discussed earlier: there's got to be a "down" or there is no "up." Unless evil existed, we couldn't know what God's goodness and grace are all about.

Once carnal man had reared his head for the first time,

we read of Adam and Eve that *"...the eyes of them both were opened and they knew that they were naked."* Can you imagine their horror as this terrible realization burst in on them? They suddenly knew there was an "up" and a "down," a "right" and a "wrong." They may or may not have had immediate knowledge of what consequences they could expect, but they knew the joy of God's presence was missing. The first moral truth they learned was the pain of disobedience. And the devil who tempted them was nowhere around to comfort them! Instead, he used their failures to condemn them.

Remember, now, God didn't tempt them to do evil. Let's look at *James 1:13-15:*

> *"Let no man say when he is tempted, I am tempted of God: for God cannot be tempted with evil, neither tempteth he any man: But every man is tempted, when he is drawn away of his own lust, and enticed. Then when lust hath conceived, it bringeth forth sin: and sin, when it is finished, bringeth forth death."*

God didn't turn His back and leave His creation alone to face the tempter. He isn't a party to temptation of His creation. Nor is He ever tempted himself to play into the hands of the evil one.

The second thing I want to establish is that temptation is brought by the devil. *I Thessalonians 3:5 says, "For this cause, when I could no longer forbear, I sent to know your faith, lest by some means the tempter have tempted you, and our labour be in vain."*

Who is the tempter, again? Look at *Matthew 4:1-3.*

These verses plainly tell us. Verse 1 says, in part, *"Then was Jesus led up of the Spirit into the wilderness to be tempted of the devil."*

I can just hear someone saying, "It looks like God and the devil teamed up on Jesus! Now remember, Brother Plunkett, you said that God didn't tempt anyone!" This verse doesn't say God tempted Jesus; it says the devil tempted Him. There's a big difference. God allowed the devil to tempt Jesus. Sometimes the devil unwittingly helps accomplish God's purpose in us. Every time he is defeated, as he was in the wilderness, his kingdom on earth is weakened and God's is strengthened.

You can rest assured that God always has our best interest at heart, even when we are tempted or when it looks like the world will fall in on us. And remember...the spirit man was always in Jesus' driver's seat when He lived on earth. Can't you hear Him talking to himself as he was carried in the Spirit's loving arms into the wilderness to start His defeat of Satan's kingdom... "It'll be rough...he'll use his best fiery arrows on me...but spirit man, We've got to do this. We've got to do it once and for all...for today, for tomorrow...for the people in Jerusalem and around the world this day and the billions yet to be born in nations that don't even exist. Right now, but stay with me. I need to feel your support. This will be a test unlike any other I've known. Stay with me, Spirit of God, and help me keep spirit man in control."

The devil tempted Christ in the same three areas as he tempted Eve. The last half of *Matthew 4:3 says, "If thou be the Son of God, command that these stones be made bread."* That is the lust of the flesh. In verse 2 of that passage of Scripture, Matthew notes that Jesus was "afterward an hungered." Just like with Eve, Satan appealed to Jesus' sense of hunger. He had been fasting for 40 days, remember, and He was hungry. He experienced the same reaction to it that you and I would experience. He was weak — and he was hungry. *"If thou be the Son of God,"* the devil taunted Him, *"command that these stones be made bread."* Jesus could have said, "I'll show you, devil, that I am the son of God." He could have made the stones turn into bread just as He later made water turn into wine at a wedding feast. And He could have eaten the bread to strengthen his natural man. But spirit man was in control. He resisted.

Then we read in verses 8 and 9 of that chapter, *"Again the devil taketh him up into an exceeding high mountain, and showeth him all the kingdoms of the world and the glory of them; and sayeth unto him, all these things will I give thee if thou wilt fall down and worship me."* It must have looked so good. But where Eve took the bait and the lust of the eyes caught her in its poisonous net, Jesus withstood the temptation and didn't yield.

There's one little side trip we'll take right here, while we're on the subject of the lust of the eye. It's something Jesus said in *Matthew 5:27,28:*

> *"Ye have heard that it hath been said by them of old time, thou shalt not commit adultery; but I say unto you, that whosoever looketh on a woman to lust after her hath committed adultery with her already in his heart."*

And remember what James said in *James 1:14...* *"But every man is tempted when he is drawn away of his own lust, and enticed,"* The sin of the man is lust, and the sin of the woman is enticement, in adulterous relationships. Eve enticed Adam...and he sinned when he lusted after what she offered.

I'm not a "clothesline preacher," and I don't believe in making women the scapegoats here, but let me state it in plain English: the women set the moral standards of the home, the dating relationships of our young people, and the nation. That doesn't mean they should wear their hemlines to the floor, their sleeves to the wrist, their hair stringing long and straight or done up in a "Pentecostal bun" on the back of their head, and no makeup. But they should be modest enough both at home and in public that the clothes they wear and the way they present themselves doesn't draw the lustful attention of every man who's still alive and breathing. By the same token, most men who are alive and breathing are going to notice any attractive woman around them. But they are doing themselves a big favor — unless that woman is their wife — if they admire her the same way they would the thundering beauty of Niagara Falls: from a safe distance, for a short time. If the woman is their wife, and the two of them are alone, that's another delightful story we won't go into here.

Now let's look at the third category in which Satan tempted first Eve and then Jesus: the pride of life. Let's look particularly at how he dealt with Jesus, as recorded in *Matthew 4:5,6:*

> *"Then the devil taketh him up into the holy city, and setteth him on a pinnacle of the temple. And saith unto him, If thou be the Son of God, cast thyself down: for*

*it is written, He shall give his angels
charge concerning thee: and in their
hands they shall bear thee up, lest at any
time thou dash thy foot against a stone."*

Here the devil is tempting Jesus in the pride of life.
"Cast yourself down." "Show off what all you can do."
"Or maybe you're not really the Son of God after all.
Prove it." The enemy had won that round with Eve, just
as he'd won all the others. Thank God, Jesus didn't suc-
cumb to that temptation or any of the rest.

Remember — the devil tempted Christ in the same
three categories in which he'd tempted Eve. If he had
had any new tricks, he certainly would have tried them
out on Jesus! But Satan's warehouse of tricks has only
these three ways to tempt us, just as he could only try
these three on Jesus and Eve. And praise God: Jesus did
not succumb to any of them! Not only did He not give
in, He passes what He learned about temptation right
along to us. In *Hebrews 4:15* we learn that "...we have
not a high priest which cannot be touched with the
feeling of our infirmities, but was tempted in all points
like as we are, yet without sin." The first Adam failed
and had to look back with regret. Thank God the "Second
Adam" didn't fail! He was living in his spirit man. Because
He won, we can win. The precedent was set in the case
of Satan versus Jesus Christ. And Christ won the battle.
Our battle!

Paul affirms this in *I Corinthians 10:13* when he records,

*"There hath no temptation taken you
but such as is common to man: but God*

49

> *is faithful, who will not suffer you to be*
> *tempted above that ye are able; but will*
> *with the temptation also make a way to*
> *escape, that ye may be able to bear it."*

Let's look at four different facts from this verse.
First...<u>there hath no temptation taken you but such as is</u>
<u>common to man.</u> Satan would have you believe that you
are the only one who has ever had to go through what
you are facing, and that no one cares or understands.
But take heart — multitudes have already gone through
the same thing. Some may have given up, but many have
come through victorious. So can you! In *I John 4:4* we
read, *"Greater is he that is in you, than he that is in*
the world." And even if no other person since then or
before then has faced what you're facing, Jesus experienced all the temptations man would ever face. And He
conquered them — for me, and for you.

Second...<u>God is faithful.</u> There is so much that can be
said about the faithfulness of God, but let's simply say
that He never fails. You can safely rely on Him in your
fiery furnace as the young Israelites did. You can rely
on Him when the waters are about to close over your
head just as Peter did. You can rely on Him in the belly
of the whale as Jonah did — even though he ended up
there because he disobeyed God in the first place. As
frosting on this piece of cake, let's look at some Scripture
passages that reassure us of His faithfulness:

> *"For sin shall not have dominion over*
> *you: for ye are not under the law, but*
> *under grace" (Romans 6:14).*

*"Submit yourselves therefore to God.
Resist the devil, and he will flee from
you." (James 4:7).*

*"The Lord knoweth how to deliver the
godly out of temptations, and to reserve
the unjust unto the day of judgment to
be punished" (II Peter 2:9).*

*"And the Lord said, Simon, Simon, be-
hold, Satan hath desired to have you, that
he may sift you as wheat: But I have
prayed for thee, that thy faith fail not:
and when thou art converted, strengthen
thy brethren" (Luke 22:31,32).*

Third, <u>God will not allow you to be tempted above
what you can stand.</u> We are to rejoice that God has
enough confidence in us that He can allow Satan to
tempt us, and enough love for us that He won't allow
anything to totally overwhelm us. And He has enough
love for the world that He will allow the testimony of
our example — when we don't fold under the pressure
— to bring other people to Him. God had a lot of confidence in an ordinary man, a long time ago, a man named
Job. In fact, God and Satan were talking about him...like
this:

*"Hast thou considered my servant Job,"
God said, "that there is none like him in
the earth, a perfect and an upright man,
one that feareth God, and escheweth
evil?" (Job 1:8).*

51

The devil replied that Job was serving God just for what he could get out of it, and if God would let him at Job for even a little while, he would make Job curse God to His face. God said to Satan, *"Job is my friend. After you have done everything to him that you can do, except take his life, I have confidence that he will still love and serve me."*

Often when people come to me for counseling I remind them what God said about Job. Then I remind them of *John 15:15* where God calls us His friends. Then I ask, "How do you know but what God and the devil have had a little chat about you, and God told Satan he could go ahead and put you through that trial you are now enduring, but just so far, and that God has enough confidence in you that He knows you will still love and serve Him when the trial has passed. And think what a testimony this will be to the people you know that maybe I could not reach, and no other preacher could ever reach, but you can reach them."

No wonder the Bible tells us to count it all joy when we fall into divers temptations! What a powerful testimony we have, once we emerge victorious on the other side, of His love. What a way to strengthen God's kingdom, as we share the testimony of how God brought us through our fiery trials

Fourth, <u>God will with the temptation make a way of escape</u>. The devil brings the temptation; God provides the escape route. The question is, are we willing to escape? Will we go...as my dad used to say, will we "git while the gittin' is good"? Let's look at *Hebrews 2:16-18* (Amplified Bible) while we consider this:

"For, as we all know, He (Christ) did

*not take hold of angels (the fallen angels)
— to give them a helping and delivering
hand; but he did take hold of (the fallen)
descendants of Abraham — to reach them
a helping and delivering hand.*

*"So it is evident that it was essential
that He be made like His brethren in every
respect, in order that he might become a
merciful (sympathetic) and faithful High
Priest in the things related to God, to
make atonement and propitiation for the
people's sins.*

*"For because He Himself (in His hu-
manity) has suffered in being tempted
(tested and tried), He is able (immediately) to run to the cry of (assist,
relieve) those who are being tempted and
tested and tried (and who therefore are
being exposed to suffering)."*

Sometimes the escape route looks impossible, and
worse than whatever the enemy has to hold over our
heads. Do you remember Moses? Here was a man leading
millions of people out of slavery toward a "Promised
Land" that only he knew about, and he finally got to that
point where we all end up sooner or later: he was between the devil and the deep blue sea. Actually, it was
the Red Sea. But did he listen to that inevitable voice of
temptation?

I can just imagine Satan there whispering in Moses'
ear. "Did you really think it would work? All you have

is a bunch of children and ignorant slave people. They've never been this far from home in their whole lives. They're so dependent on the handouts from their slave masters in Egypt...even though they have been meager at best...they'll starve to death. If they don't drown or die at the hands of those screaming Egyptian charioteers hot on your heels. Think it over, Moses...while there's time to turn back into slavery. It's better than drowning in this churning sea...or being pierced through with Egyptian arrows...or watching all these people starve in the hot desert when your God lets you down. Think about it, Moses. While there's still time."

Moses called on his unfailing God. He shattered temptation into a million glistening droplets with the staff God had placed in his hand as he struck the sea waves and God parted them to reveal dry ground. God made the invisible path visible. It was there all the time. Moses just couldn't see it until he decided to do things God's way...whatever that way may be.

Remember, now, the temptations you are facing have been faced — and conquered — before. In the wilderness and at Calvary. God is faithful to see you through them. He won't allow the enemy to tempt you in a way you can't withstand. And, when temptation comes, He will make a way of escape when your life is firmly in His hand, with the spirit man firmly in control.

Chapter 5
"Sweet Uses of Adversity"

Everybody has a "Miss Jones" lurking somewhere in the past — you know, the school teacher who went around quoting poems no 15-year-old wants to memorize...and Shakespeare's plays...the Miss Jones at my school used to quote a lot from Shakespeare about the blessing in disguise that adversity was. It went like this:

> *"Sweet are the uses of adversity,*
> *Which like the toad, ugly and venomous,*
> *Wears yet a precious jewel in his head;*
> *And this our life, exempt from public haunt,*
> *Finds tongues in trees, books in the*
> *   running brooks,*
> *Sermons in stones, and good in everything."*
> *   "As You Like It," Act II, Scene I*

When the carnal man stays in the driver's seat of your

life, you will fail and sin over and over again and never ask for forgiveness. If the natural man remains in the driver's seat, you will worry yourself to death. Like the star subject in a little poem I read many years ago:

> *"The worry cow would have lasted 'til*
> *   now,*
> *If she hadn't lost her breath;*
> *But she thought her hay wouldn't last*
> *   all day,*
> *So she choked herself to death."*

When the spirit man is in the driver's seat of your life, most of the time you will succeed at Christian living.

The next three chapters of this book deal with the natural man and our struggles with him. For the purpose of this discussion, we will use the words mind, intellect, and personality synonymously and interchangeably (see Chart #3.)

It is in the area of the natural man, the soul, that we often have so many unmanageable problems. We need to learn how to handle them so they will become blessings and not destroy us. You see, it is not our problems that make or break us, but our reaction to them. We have to look, deep within ourselves in our spirit man, to find the "sermons in stones" and "books in the running brooks" and the "good in everything." In that deep part of us that's "exempt from public haunt." Adversity is like a storm. It drives some ships to destruction and others to the harbor. It causes some men to be bitter; others, better. It is the set of the sail, and not the force of the gale, that determines the way we go.

Time forces a physical maturity on a person, unless

56

he is deformed in some way, but it doesn't force a mental, emotional, or spiritual maturity on anyone. Many physical adults are emotional cripples; they have not matured in the area of the mind or the personality. These people cannot handle life. Every little thing that comes into their lives becomes a major catastrophe.

In the *Song of Solomon 2:15*, King Solomon said, *"Take us the foxes, the little foxes, that spoil the vines."* Solomon knew something was eating his grapes. No doubt he was looking at his vineyard one day, thinking about how many grapes he was losing, and he saw the big foxes sitting on the ground. They were watching the progress of the little foxes Solomon saw as he looked up into the vines and saw the student destroyers sitting there eating the ripening grapes.

He realized the tender vines would not support the weight of the adult foxes, but the little foxes had no problem jumping from vine to vine, getting where the grapes were hanging luscious and ripe. It was the little foxes doing the damage.

Our lives are likewise not made up of big events, for the most part, but they consist of little things. We get up, drive across town to work, go home, have dinner, read the paper, go to the store, sleep, go to church, and other routine things. The "little foxes" can creep into these ordinary events of life and spoil our jobs...our home life...our sleep...our friendships and worship experiences at church...and meanwhile the big foxes are sitting there. Sometimes they take a leap into the vines as well.

Perhaps you're having an experience like that right now. Perhaps you are going through a hard trial and God is trying to work out something in you or through you, and you can't understand it. It's like looking at the underneath side of embroidery — you can only see the knots and tangled threads. But when you come out the other end of it, and see it the way God sees it, you can see the silken tapestry He has made of your life and you will understand. The side the rest of the world has been seeing is golden threads carefully woven by the Master Weaver. The knots and tangles are a secret between Him and you. Sometimes you can help another Christian who is struggling by telling that person about the knots and scars — and showing them by your life that God has placed a jewel in your personal "toad of adversity."

I am reminded of the man who had a wonderful wife who did everthing she could to please him. One night, as they started to bed, she asked him, "Darling, what would you like for breakfast in the morning?"

He replied, "I want two eggs: one scrambled and the other one fried." The next morning, she prepared his eggs and put them in front of him on the table with toast and coffee, but he just sat there and frowned.

When his wife asked him what was wrong, he replied, "You scrambled the wrong egg!"

Some people are like that — never happy with anything. That is because they are unhappy with themselves. They have not learned to accept life, and they are trying to reason out and rearrange everything that comes their way. If you find yourself in this category, remember that you can't change the facts of your life. They exist, unalterable, and that will never change. But you <u>can</u> change the way they affect you and how you let yourself feel about them. Let's re-read *Genesis 1:26,27* together:

> *"And God said, Let us make man in*
> *our image, after our likeness: and let*

*them have dominion over the fish of the
sea, and over the fowl of the air, and over
the cattle, and over all the earth, and over
every creeping thing that creepeth upon
the earth."*

*"So God created man in his own image,
in the image of God created he him; male
and female created he them."*

In an even closer look at verse 26, the word "God"
comes from the Hebrew word "Elohim," meaning <u>more
than one</u>. Basically, it refers to a <u>triune God</u>, one Godhead
made up of three distinct personalities: God the Father,
God the Son, and God the Holy Spirit, like the three
sides of an equilateral triangle. All are equal parts of the
whole Godhead being. When God made man in His
image, then, He also made man to have three parts: man
is a spirit (spirit man), man is an intellectual being (natural man), and he lives in a fleshly body (carnal man).
Like God, man is a <u>tri-unity</u>; <u>tri</u> meaning three, and <u>uni</u>
meaning one. He is one individual. He has three parts.

Keeping this in mind, and especially the natural man,
who is the subject of this chapter, let's take an imaginary
trip to a place in the Rocky Mountains known as the
"Continental Divide." A plaque on one of those majestic
peaks announces to the world that this is the great divide
of North America. If a drop of water falls on the edge of
this plaque and is split in half, one half will eventually
make its way into the Atlantic Ocean. The other half will
end up in the Pacific Ocean. The entire Rocky Mountain
chain is a natural watershed. It divides the direction

water flows — to the east or the west.

Likewise, our mind (the natural man) is the continental divide of the human being. The mind is also the seat of our will and our emotions. It is in this watershed area of our life that our major decisions are made. On one side of this personal "divide" is the spirit man; on the other, the carnal man. When we hear the Word of God taught or preached, it is here that the decision is made as to which way the Word will flow. The natural man may decide to reject the tugging of spirit man and discard what he hears. It flows out onto the jagged carnal man and is evaporated by doubt and unbelief. Let's look at *Hebrews 3:14-4:3* for another way to understand this truth.

> *"For we are made partakers of Christ, if we hold the beginning of our confidence stedfast unto the end; While it is said, Today if ye will hear his voice, harden not your hearts, as in the provocation.*

> *"For some, when they had heard did provoke: howbeit not all that came out of Egypt by Moses. But with whom was he grieved forty years? Was it not with them that had sinned, whose carcases fell in the wilderness? And to whom sware he that they should not enter into his rest, but to them that believed not?"*

> *"So we see that they could not enter in because of unbelief. Let us therefore fear,*

lest, a promise being left us of entering into his rest, any of you should seem to come short of it."

"For unto us was the gospel preached, as well as unto them: but the word preached did not profit them, not being mixed with faith in them that heard it. For we which have believed do enter into rest, as he said, As I have sworn in my wrath, if they shall enter into my rest: although the works were finished from the foundation of the world."

Now look closely at Chapter 4, verse 2. The gospel was preached, but it did not profit those who heard it because it was not mixed with faith. What a tragedy! Every Sabbath Pastor Moses preached the Word of God to those people as they journeyed from Egypt to the Promised Land. But when they heard the Word of God, it flowed out toward the carnal man, got caught on the rocky terrain of self, and was evaporated by doubt.

When Pastor Moses finally got his congregation to the very gates of the Promised Land, he sent in twelve spies, and ten of them came back saying they could not possibly take the land. The people in there were giants, they said, and the Israelites mere <u>grasshoppers</u> by comparison!

But two of the spies, Joshua and Caleb, said, "WE CAN TAKE IT!" You see, when they heard the Word, it flowed a different direction. It flowed into their spirit man because they made the decision to believe what God had said. Forty years later, after wandering around and around in the desert, Israel came back to the border of

61

the Promised Land again. Now they were ready to go in and possess it. But God said, "Hold it! Only <u>two</u> of you above 19 years of age are going to enter into My rest. The rest of you, back into the desert. All I could hear out of you was how your mouths watered for the onions, the leeks, the garlic, the cucumbers, and the flesh pots — the false securities and rest — of Egypt. Now go back to Egypt — but go without My help!" *Hebrews 3:17* says that their carcases fell in the wilderness. Young mothers and fathers had to hand their infant babies to teenagers because they couldn't go in. Their bones bleached on the desert sand.

Joshua and Caleb took a bunch of infants, children, adolescents, and older teenagers, and conquered the Promised Land. What a testimony to the enthusiasm of new Christians — those babes in Christ we so often speak of. They're the ones with all the fire!

Well, when the Word of God falls on our mind and the decision is made to believe it, then it flows down into our spirit man and becomes a life-enriching part of us. Remember — the mind is the seat of the intellect, the dividing line between spirit man and carnal man (see Chart #4). As long as you keep the intellect and the emotions separated, the intellect wins out every time. But if you let your intellect and emotions come into contact, emotion almost always wins out. Emotion, directed by the carnal man, short-circuits the system and circumvents your intellect.

It is in this area that man becomes a civil war within himself. When temptation falls on the mind, if it flows toward the carnal man, emotion gets the upper hand and it is so easy to commit that tempting sin. But God showed me the defense we have against this! *Isaiah*

59:19b says, "When the enemy shall come in like a flood, the Spirit of the Lord shall lift up a standard against him." When we hear the Word of God and the decision is made to receive it and believe it, then it flows down into our spirit man and becomes a part of us, as I have already pointed out. Then, when temptation rushes and the enemy comes in like a flood, but we reject the temptation, the temptation flows toward our spirit man. The Spirit of the Lord that is in our spirit man sees it coming and raises up a bulwark — a flood wall — a standard out of the Word that has become a part of us. Instead of the temptation overcoming us, it beats itself out against the flood wall. Hallelujah! And how much better it is to fortify ourselves in advance against the flood we know is eventually coming, rather than trying to erect a hasty sandbag levee after the flood waters start over the river's banks!

I am not interested in just helping you rearrange your problems; I want you to learn how to overcome them and be victorious. It is in the area of the soul, or the mind, that so many Christians have problems. You might have thought that you wouldn't have any problems after you gave your life to Christ. That is precisely what the devil wants you to think. Listen to the words of Jesus in *John 16:33, "These things have I spoken unto you, that in me ye might have peace. In the world ye shall have tribulation; but be of good cheer; I have overcome the world."*

The devil wants you to think God isn't interested in your problems, but that's a lie. I wouldn't give a snap of my fingers for a religion that only offered me hope in the hereafter; I need help right here and now. And it is here and now — in preparation for the hereafter —

where God wants to help us!

There are many verses that promise God's help in this life, but I will mention just a few. In Genesis, the very first book of the Bible, Hagar brings the plight of a single mother raising a child alone to her God when she sits down out of earshot of the hungry child and talks to God: "Don't let me have to watch him starve to death!" And she cried and talked to God about the frustrations of single parenthood. *Genesis 21:17* records God's reaction to her plea, *"And God heard the voice of the lad; and the angel of God called to Hagar out of heaven, and said unto her, What aileth thee, Hagar? Fear not; for God hath heard the voice of the lad where he is."* God promised her the boy would survive, their needs would be met, and he would make Ishmael's descendants a great nation. *"God opened her eyes,"* a later verse says, *"and she saw a well of water; and she went, and filled the bottle with water, and gave the lad to drink. And God was with the lad; and he grew, and dwelt in the wilderness, and became an archer."*

> *"But I am poor and needy; yet the Lord thinketh upon me: thou art my help and my deliverer; make no tarrying, O my God" (Psalm 40:17).*

> *"And it shall come to pass, that before they call, I will answer; and while they are yet speaking, I will hear" (Isaiah 65:24).*

> *"God is our refuge and strength, a very present help in trouble" (Psalm 46:1).*

> *"Let us therefore come boldly unto the throne of grace, that we may obtain mercy, and find grace to help in time of need" (Hebrews 4:16).*

There are a number of reasons why people lose out with God. Let me give you a few. First of all, they don't understand themselves. They are at civil war within themselves and the sides desperately need reconciling. Second, they don't really understand what they are going through. Third, people often don't know how to appropriate God's Word to their daily lives. Fourth, we often forget that *Romans 8:28* assures us that there is a lesson to be learned and something good to be found in every trial. We just have to learn to look at life that way. Fifth, the natural man cannot understand spiritual things. Let's look at *I Corinthians 2:14*, which says,

> *"But the natural man receiveth not the things of the Spirit of God: for they are foolishness unto him: neither can he know them, because they are spiritually discerned."*

That means they are understood only by our spirit man. The natural man tries to reason them out, and when he cannot, he discards them. He throws the baby out with the bath water, so to speak. Look at *John 6:59,60...*

> *"These things said he in the synagogue, as he taught in Capernaum. Many therefore of his disciples, when they had heard this, said, This is an hard saying; who can hear it?"*

Jesus, by a great miracle, had just the day before fed a multitude of people with one little boy's sack lunch. Then he tried to use what he had just done for them physically to teach them a great spiritual lesson. But in verses 41 and 42, the Jews murmur at Him because He claims to be the Bread which came down from heaven, and they say He is Jesus, the son of Joseph. How then could He have come down from heaven? When the natural man could not understand this great spiritual lesson, many of the disciples turned away and walked no more with Him.

In *John 21:15-17* we see another example of Jesus teaching by the use of a parable — something the listeners can understand — to explain spiritual truths. Simon Peter was not capable, at this point, of receiving into his spirit man what Christ was trying to teach him. Let's look at that passage of Scripture.

> *"So when they had dined, Jesus saith to Simon Peter, Simon, son of Jonas, lovest thou me more than these? He saith unto him, Yea, Lord; thou knowest that I love thee. He saith unto him, Feed my lambs."*

> *"He saith to him again the second time, Simon, son of Jonas, lovest thou me? He saith unto him, Yea, Lord; thou knowest that I love thee. He saith unto him, Feed my sheep."*

> *"He saith unto him the third time, Simon, son of Jonas, lovest thou me? Peter*

*was grieved because he said unto him the
third time, Lovest thou me? And he said
unto him, Lord, thou knowest all things:
thou knowest that I love thee. Jesus saith
unto him, Feed my sheep."*

In trying to develop His relationship with Peter on a
much deeper level, Jesus used the word "agape" love
for love in verses 15 and 16. Agape is the God-kind of
love. It is love without condition; love that flows from
our spirit man. It makes us love our enemies. It makes
us do good to them that hate us and pray for them that
despitefully use us.

Jesus said to Peter, *"If you really have that God-given,
unconditional kind of love, use it to feed my sheep.
Even that one that's so hard to love. You know, Peter,
a lot of people might find you hard to love. But I love
you. Unconditionally. You love the unlovable people
in your world the same way."*

In these same two verses, however, Peter is using a
different word for love. He uses the word that we would
translate "brotherly love." It's the Greek word <u>phileo</u>. In
essence, Peter was saying, "Lord, you know I love you
the way I'd love a friend or a brother." When Jesus
persisted, the Scripture says Peter got his feelings hurt
because he thought Jesus doubted his love of friendship.

When Jesus saw that Peter couldn't comprehend the
new dimension to which He was trying to take their
relationship, then He used the same word for love in
verse 17 that Peter was using. He said, *"Peter, if you
love me, if you are truly my friend and my brother,
then feed my sheep."*

Now, all the while that natural man is "dividing" what

falls on his life and sending it to the spirit man or the carnal man, he is doing this job with both his conscious and subconscious mind (see Chart #5).

Psychologists tell us that everything we ever see and hear is recorded in the subconscious, although not all of it is consciously remembered. A child can hear before it is born. One experiment which proved this was when researchers attached a bell to the stomach of a pregnant woman, and every time the baby kicked they rang the bell. After a period of time, they would ring the bell first and then the baby would kick. The baby had been conditioned to connect kicking and the sound of the bell. It could hear — and respond to — noises from outside the womb.

Now suppose mom is expecting little Susie or Junior, and there is always a big fuss going on around the house. That little subconscious mind records all of that fuss. Is it any wonder, then, that Susie or Junior comes into the world a nervous wreck from birth?

As the baby grows older, his subconscious mind becomes overloaded and starts trying to relieve itself by pushing some of the things that are bothering it up into the doorway of the conscious mind where that conscious mind can create an explanation that the person can live with. This is its only avenue of relief. Without you realizing it, when this happens, your conscious mind scrutinizes it. If it decides this memory will hurt you and be painful if it becomes a conscious thought, it pushes the painful memory back into the subconscious again. Perhaps the next time it will surface in a crazy, mixed-up dream. Psychologists call this <u>conversion reaction</u>, when the subconscious mind tries to find some avenue of relief for the painful events stored there —

other than bringing them into the conscious mind so they can be dealt with properly.

If this is the condition of your natural mind, and if you don't seek help from a Godly counselor who can help you identify and handle your problem, you are a good candidate for a mental breakdown such as I had when I was just 16 years of age. You don't have to live a long time to experience a lot of pain...it can happen at any age.

Oftentimes it is hard for a psychiatrist or psychologist to help you, unless they are born again and can help you put your faith to work to restore those "locust years" the enemy has stolen from you *(Joel 2:25)*. You can't physically remember things that happened to you before you learned to talk — even as far back as when you were in your mother's womb — because words are your tools for remembering and you can't remember farther back than the time when you learned to talk. However, many of your hurts have been in place from long before you could talk and you need that supernatural help to bring them to light for healing.

This is where our relationship with Christ makes a difference. God doesn't want to save just enough of us so we can go to heaven, although that is the most important part of salvation. He wants to help us with our problems in this life so that we can have that "more abundant life" *(John 10:10)*. He wants us to have an enjoyable time on the way! Can you imagine getting on an airplane and hearing the pilot say, "Ladies and gentlemen, I know we'll make it to the city of our destination today, but probably just by the barest margin of safety. We have just enough fuel, and just enough air pressurization equipment, and just one cup of coffee per passenger, and no lunches...but don't worry. With a good tail wind and no storms, we should get there without too awful much trouble." No! We expect to hear the pilot say, "Welcome aboard! You're flying the best, most modern, well-equipped, well-stocked airplane available. All systems are operating perfectly, dinner is ready to be served, and you'll arrive at your destination on time in perfect comfort. Enjoy your trip."

Isaiah 9:6 talks about the One called "Wonderful...Counsellor..." who can reach back into your past...and my past...and help us bring our hurts to the "Prince of Peace" for healing. His name is Jesus, and the Bible says in *John 2:25b, "He knew what was in man."*

Thank God, Jesus knows by the power of the Holy Spirit what is in our hearts and lives. He can reach back to the very moment of conception if need be and heal every wound. In place of the bitterness He can bring forgiveness. In place of resentment, He offers sweetness...acceptance of self and others. In place of hatred He offers love.

Jesus may use your pastor, a friend, or a Christian counselor to help you reach what you can reach. Thank Him for that. Beyond that, He will reach His hand of love into the recesses of your battered heart and perform emotional surgeries far beyond the reach of man.

Jesus said, in *John 8:32, "Ye shall know the truth, and the truth shall make you free."* Before we can be free of the pain or sin we knowingly carry around with us, we have to face the truth about ourselves. That is often the hardest part of such an emotional healing. We don't want to admit we are carrying around hatred, bitterness, or resentment against our family or friends. Or even ourself. Or sometimes against God himself. Jacob came to that place where he was willing to face up to the source of his problems...good old Jacob himself, as it turned out. He had wrestled with an angel all night seeking peace for his troubled spirit and finally the angel had had enough. He said to Jacob, I'm leaving. Enough already."

Jacob grabbed him by a wing or a sandal strap and said, "Oh, no, you aren't going. I can't live like this any longer. I can't stand this kind of torment. I've got to have help. I've got to have it now. This night."

The angel faced Jacob and said, *"What is thy name?"* *(Genesis 32:27)*. When Jacob answered that question, he knew the source of his trouble. His name meant <u>deceiver, supplanter</u>. He met his problems head-on, conquered them, and felt the peace of God return to his life.

I once read of a Chinese philosopher who said, "He who conquers others is strong...but he who conquers himself is MIGHTY."

Chapter 6
Reinforcements!

The Bible sounds a solemn warning in *I Peter 5:8* (Amplified Version):

> *"Be well-balanced — temperate, sober-minded; be vigilant and cautious at all times, for that enemy of yours, the devil, roams around like a lion roaring (in fierce hunger), seeking someone to seize upon and devour."*

In *Matthew 12:43-45*, Jesus talked about the devil also.

> *"When the unclean spirit is gone out of a man, he walketh through dry places, seeking rest, and findeth none. Then he saith, I will return into my house from whence I came out: and when he is come, he findeth it empty, swept, and garnished.*

"Then goeth he, and taketh with himself seven other spirits more wicked than himself, and they enter in and dwell there: and the last state of that man is worse than the first. Even so shall it be also unto this wicked generation."

In these verses, Jesus told the story of a man who had gotten saved; He also talked about how the devil had to get out when the man got saved. The unclean spirit had to leave, and he had no choice. Christ and the devil could not and still cannot live together in the same house. The unclean spirit roamed through "dry places." He was seeking something to feed on — some place to rest. He found nothing so he went back to the house (man) from which he had come out. He found the house empty. He found it clean. Swept out. Put in order. The person's life was empty of sin. But it wasn't filled up with much of the joy, peace, or contentment of Christ yet. It had some love...some joy...but not the life filling kind Christ was longing to place there. Something was still dangerously wrong in that house...even when it seemed so right. It was empty of sin...but it was dangerously empty.

If we could pull the curtain back and see beyond the physical realm, we might have witnessed this diabolical scene. Picture if you will...

The unclean spirit goes to a convention of demons. He has found no rest outside the house (man) from which he's been evicted. But there's still room for him there, he thinks. He tries to sneak in the back door of the convention as Lucifer stands screaming at the other demons cowed fearfully in front of him. Unclean develops a case of shaky knees.

Satan sees him slip in the back door and points a flaming finger in his direction. Fiery arrows lunge at the demon's quivering heart. "What are you doing here? I thought I sent you to possess Mr. Natural Man! Give me an account of yourself. It better be fast — and it better be good!"

By now every leering eye in the room is on Unclean as he answers in a trembling voice, "I was living there until a few days ago, but Natural Man accepted Jesus into his heart and I had to...". Before he can finish the sentence, Satan shrieks at him until all of hell shakes.

"Don't ever say that name again in my presence! I hate it! I hate it! I can't stand to hear it!" The edges of his voice are tinged with fear.

As the brimstone walls glow with reflected fury, another demon stands up to address Lucifer. "My name is Discouragement. If you will give me permission to go with Unclean, we will go together to Natural Man. I will help work a few barbs into him to get him discouraged. Maybe I'll have another person in his church say something nasty about him."

A second demon stands to speak. "My name is Depression. If you let me go with Unclean and Discouragement, just about the time things start going wrong I'll get him to look at all the negative things in his life and get him all depressed. A little extra salt in the wound would do him no harm."

A third demon stands. His name is Defeat. "Let me go, too! When things are at a low point I'll step in and create a real mess on his job. You know how much he depends on that job. If that doesn't work, I'll make the baby spill milk on his suit Sunday morning at breakfast. He'll scream at the baby, the baby will cry, his wife will get upset, and a grand and glorious argument will get started. I'll keep it going until it's too late to go to church, and he'll be ready to quit. He'll be defeated. Maybe he'll never go back to church again!"

Excitement is beginning to build. The fourth demon jumps to his feet and claps his hands with glee. "My name is Jealousy! When Discouragement, Depression, and Defeat go with Unclean, let me go too! When Natural Man gets really defeated and starts missing chruch, I'll get him looking at other people instead of the Word of God and point out to him how good other Christians seem to have it compared to him and in spite of the way they sometimes live. You know — the way they get the position he wanted in church, and the praise he never got for fixing the furnace at that place last year. I'll remind him that even the pastor never thanks him for anything he does. But he always manages to thank the new guy — from the platform, no less! I'll make him so jealous he won't <u>ever</u> get over it!"

The fifth demon jumps up with a sneering grin on his face. "My name is Criticism and I want to go, too! I'll get him to start criticizing just a little bit, with just a little sarcasm thrown in for good measure, and pretty soon he'll be attacking everybody and everything. Of course, I'll make sure some people criticize him regularly, too. 'Sauce for the goose is sauce for the gander', you know."

The sixth demon stands to offer his services. "Don't forget me. I'm the spirit of Judgment. After Natural Man has been overcome by the criticism offered about him by others, I'll cause him to start passing judgment on them. I'll even make him say that the whole bunch of them are nothing but hypocrites and they ought to go — well, they ought to come home with me and Brother Criticism, here, if you know what I mean."

Finally a big, sour-looking demon pulls himself up. In a hateful, steady, seasoned voice he begins to speak. "My name is Destruction. This plan of action against Natural Man sounds good to me. I'd like to offer the crowning touch. Just as he starts tottering on the brink of the abyss, and thinks there might be one last slim chance he'll survive, I'll come in for the kill and finish him off. Sort of a 'last resort' for these other six fellows here, you might say. I'm the one they save for last."

Suddenly, the house of Natural Man (his life) was full of fury seven times greater than before. Where did it start? How did it happen? It started in an empty corner of Natural Man's mind with the first thought of discouragement. It happened step by step, and he didn't realize it because he wasn't watching or directing where those precious drops from God's Word were going. Uncleanness...Depression...Discouragement...Defeat...Jealousy...Criticism...Judgment...Destruction. Natural Man gave in by getting careless and before long his mind was under the sway of Satan's tormenting spirits. Remember, Jesus said in *Matthew 12* that the unclean spirit went and found seven devils worse than himself. We often take that to mean that they were demons of murder and robbery and the like, but that's not so. The devil is too smart for that. He couldn't tempt very many people that way. But they came in and hit Natural Man where he was most vulnerable...on the sly...unnoticed...like the little foxes that spoiled Solomon's vineyards and ate his grapes. One of Satan's greatest weapons is this kind of anonymous camouflage. He remains well hidden until

76

he is exposed or in control of a person's life. By the time it becomes that obvious, his death-grip is all the harder to escape.

> *"Do you not know that if you continually surrender yourselves to anyone to do His will, you are the slaves of him whom you obey, whether that be to sin, which leads to death, or to obedience which leads to righteousness — right doing and right standing with God?"*
>
> *(Romans 6:16)*

You cannot sin without first surrending your will and desires to want to do a certain thing; likewise, you cannot and will not live righteously unless you desire to do so. In the struggle between flesh and the spirit, the battleground is the mind. It is in the area of the mind that we win or lose the battles of life. There is no draw. The rain falls on the watershed of our mind and goes to one side or the other. It cannot sit on the fence.

In *II Corinthians 2:11,* Paul said, *"Lest Satan should get an advantage of us, for we are not ignorant of his devices."* But often we as Christians are ignorant of the devil's devices. The reason the unclean spirit and his seven cohorts could overcome the man Jesus told about in *Matthew 12* was because that man was ignorant of the devil's tricks and careless in his Christian life. He left some holes to be filled. The devil filled them neatly. In deadly fashion. It started out, no doubt, like it does with so many Christians.

A small incident "happened." He didn't exercise the authority he had in Jesus Christ to bind it and get rid of it. Then he was the victim of another "incident." And on and on until he was overcome.

As I have read the story of Job over and over again, one thing stands out clearly to me. Satan could not defeat Job and make him criticize God and everyone else because Satan could not defeat Job in his mind — his thinking.

A person's relationship with God is often balanced precariously on just emotional experience. Emotion is good, but not when it is allowed to dominate our life, and rule spirit man. Emotion is fickle. If you happen to get up some morning, walking with God strictly on the basis of your emotions, and suddenly you don't "feel saved," the devil can defeat you. Sometimes I don't "feel saved." But I know that I am because my relationship with God is based on His Word and what His Son did for me at Calvary, not on my emotions. I cannot allow my emotions to overtake my spirit man. Rather, my spirit man must hold the reins of my emotions. When that happens, my relationship with God is on solid footing. God is in control. I know I am saved because of what He has done for me, not because of the way I feel at any given moment. When I feel good, when life is meeting or exceeding my expectations, He helps me enjoy life even more than I could without Him at the helm. And when life is painful for me, I can still know I am saved because of what He has done for me and like David I can say, *"For I shall yet praise him, who is the health of my countenance, and my God" (Psalm 42:11).*

An old man once told me, "I have had a lot of trouble in my life — most of which never happened!" What he was trying to tell me was that he was always pulling the coattails of tomorrow's troubles today, saying, "Wait for me!" He worried so much about tomorrow and the things that might have happened, he missed out on today.

He was like the toad of adversity who coudn't see the jewel in his forehead...all he could see were the warts and bumps. Instead of sermons and books and good in everything, he focused on the stones and rushing brooks and adversities of life. But that's just the opposite of what God has planned for us!

Chapter 7
Dining with the best
<u>pigs</u> in town?

A circuit-riding preacher regularly went into a little community in the Ozark Mountains to minister. Every fourth Sunday he'd tie up his faithful horse outside the Green Valley Church and minister to the faithful gathered there. After the service one Sunday, an old mountain man invited him home for dinner. While they were sitting at the table, the farmer's pet pig under the table kept rooting around by the preacher's leg. Every now and then the circuit-rider thought he felt old porker take a bite out of his pants leg. And he was mighty close to touching skin and shin. Finally the preacher said to the old man, with just a touch of suppressed anger in his voice, "Say, feller, that's a right friendly pig you have under the table there...."

"That's just 'cause you're eatin' out of <u>his</u> bowl," the mountaineer answered, without missing a beat of his Sunday dinner. Now, friend, that preacher had a real problem. And he didn't know what to do with it. He was eatin' out of the wrong bowl. He was like a lot of people in life — programmed toward the pig trough and uncertain how to get out of that rut.

While we're still little children, we are programmed for life. Half of everything we'll ever know is already known to us by the time we start to school at the age of six. Sometimes it's good programming, and often it isn't. Our prisons are full of little boys and girls in big bodies who were programmed wrong somewhere along the line. Society is trying to deprogram and reprogram them. But the prisons and correction system are falling far short in their attempts. The recidivism, or repeat offense, rate is over 90 percent. One reason our prison systems fall so far short of the goal is that you can't beat, regiment, or legislate the hurt and sin out of an individual. Two years on a rock pile and three meals a day won't clean him up from the inside out. God alone can do that, just like God alone can reach deep into the heart of a banker...a clerk in the grocery store...a mail carrier...an independent businessman...a janitor...a school teacher... or a confused 16-year-old boy wandering the backwoods of Louisiana and heal the deep hurts in those lives. He is patiently waiting to "deprogram" our hurts and "reprogram" us for victorious living to help increase His kingdom, spend eternity with him, and enjoy life both now and in the hereafter.

While the computer language of programming is new, the idea certainly isn't. Paul wrote more than once about having to do this: he called it "putting off the old man and putting on the new..." and "forgetting those things which are behind and reaching forward to those things that are before..." and wanting to do good even at the same moment he was doing something he knew he shouldn't do.

In one of his letters to a group of New Testament believers, Paul wrote: *"Let this mind be in you, which was also in Christ Jesus" (Philippians 2:5)*. Later he wrote:

> *"Let your moderation be known unto all men. The Lord is at hand. Be careful for nothing; but in every thing by prayer and supplication with thanksgiving let your requests be made known unto God. And the peace of God, which passeth all understanding, shall keep your hearts and minds through Christ Jesus.*
>
> *"Finally, brethren, whatsoever things are true, whatsoever things are honest, whatsoever things are just, whatsoever things are pure, whatsoever things are lovely, whatsoever things are of good report; if there be any virtue, and if there be any praise, think on these things.*
>
> *"These things, which ye have both learned, and received, and heard, and seen in me, do: and the God of peace shall be with you" (Philippians 4:5-9).*

There is a difference in <u>being at peace with God</u> and <u>having the peace of God</u>. Peace <u>with</u> God is for the spirit man; the peace <u>of</u> God is for the natural man. It's for the human mind (see Chart #1). *Romans 5:1 says, "There-*

fore being justified by faith, we have peace with God through our Lord Jesus Christ." All born again Christians have peace <u>with</u> God, but not all have the peace <u>of</u> God. Many Christians don't even know there is one kind of peace for the spirit man and another for the natural man in our relationship with God.

So often Christians feel that they really <u>should</u> have peace of mind, but they don't. Instead, they are troubled and nervous. The peace they expected to find when they gave their life to Christ isn't there, even though they know that if they died they would go to heaven. They have made peace with God...and their sins are forgiven...but they have no peace when it comes to the responsibilities and trials of everyday life.

People like this are on their way to heaven. But they're seasick most of the time. Every little wave makes them "seafoam green" around the edges. God has a better plan. He wants you to spend eternity with Him and enjoy the time you spend getting there. He's the best travel agent I know of — He paid the cost of your trip to heaven, He sends your own heavenly travel companions, he wants you to enjoy the earthly preparation time you spend before your actual voyage, and once you get there you're there for eternity in His presence.

When you have a miserable trip, and get seasick too much of the time, then it's time to look hard at the disease, not just the symptom. It's time to "deprogram" and "reprogram." And that goes on and on. Whether you are saint or sinner, there's a battle between good and evil taking place in your mind. All the time. If you're a sinner, every time you hear the gospel message preached there's a voice telling you in a still, small way, "Come to Jesus. Rest. Take the good I have to offer you. I've

83

got a better way than the pain you're living in." And at the same time, another voice says to you, "Why do it today? You have plenty of time. Wait until next week." *Romans 7:18-21 says,*

> *"For I know that nothing good dwells within me, that is, in my flesh. I can will what is right, but I cannot perform it. — I have the intention and urge to do what is right, but no power to carry it out;*

> *"For I fail to practice the good deeds I desire to do, but the evil deeds that I do not desire to do are what I am (ever) doing.*

> *"Now if I do what I do not desire to do, it is no longer I doing it — it is not myself that acts — but the sin (principle) which dwells within me (fixed and operating in my soul).*

> *"So I find it to be a law (of my being) that when I want to do what is right and good, evil is ever present with me and I am subject to its insistent demands."*

Do you see how the apostle Paul was torn between good and evil? In verse 20 he said it was the sin principle, or the ability to sin, which was fixed and operating in his soul (his mind). Now take a close look at verse 22, where he said, *"For I endorse and delight in the law of God in my inmost self, with my new nature."* That is

84

his spirit man that delights in the law of God, for this is where the nature of God dwells within us. He continues in verses 23-25.

> *"But I discern in my bodily members, in the sensitive appetites and wills of the flesh, a different law at war against the law of my mind"* — now his mind has teamed up with his spirit man — *"and making me a prisoner to the law of sin that dwells in my bodily organs, in the sensitive appetites and wills of the flesh. O unhappy and pitiable and wretched man that I am! Who will release and deliver me from this body of death? O thank God. He will! through Jesus Christ."*

Mary and Martha are good examples of what I am talking about, in the story recorded in the tenth chapter of Luke. Martha had peace <u>with</u> God, but not the peace <u>of</u> God. She was so busy and troubled over preparing something for Christ to eat. Mary had both peace <u>with</u> God and the peace <u>of</u> God. She was not worried about food. She wanted to sit and bask in the Master's glow, at His feet, and learn of Him. Jesus told Martha that Mary had chosen the better part. His Word tells us how we can have that same peace <u>of</u> God. Let us go back again to the two passages of Scripture we read at the beginning of this chapter, *Philippians 2:5 and 4:6-9.*

Philippians 2:6 says, "Let this mind be in you, which was also in Christ Jesus." How do we accomplish this? *Philippians 4:6-9 tells us how.* Let's read it together:

85

> *"Be careful for"* — worried about — *"nothing; but in every thing by prayer and supplication with thanksgiving let your requests be made known unto God. And the peace of God, which passeth all understanding, shall keep your hearts and minds through Christ Jesus."*

> *"Finally, brethren, whatsoever things are true, whatsoever things are honest, whatsoever things are just, whatsoever things are pure, whatsoever things are lovely, whatsoever things are of good report; if there be any virtue, and if there be any praise, think on these things."*

> *"Those things, which ye have both learned, and received, and heard, and seen in me, do: and the God of peace shall be with you."*

The Scripture plainly speaks in verse 7 of the "peace of God," and in verse 9 it speaks of the "God of peace." Sandwiched in between these two gems in verse 8, the Holy Spirit showed me there are eight things listed for us to do. If we will do them, we will have both the God of peace and the peace of God. Let's look at them individually and discover just where we find this marvelous peace of God. It's ours when we "think on" or rest our mind on:

1. Whatsoever things are true. That means whatever is not concealed, or doesn't have to remain covered up.

2. Honest. Conduct that deserves esteem.

3. Just. Perfect agreement between your nature and your actions.

4. Pure. Whatever is of unmixed substances. You can't mix truth with lies.

5. Lovely. Whatever is pleasing and agreeable. I have met some Christians who, when you leave their presence, leave you feeling like you need a spiritual "bath" because they are so critical and grouchy. You feel like you need to go home and get a good hot bath with God's own brand of the good old lye soap grandma used to make.

6. Good report. That which is beneficial in its effect.

7. If there be any virtue.... Think on the virtue, the moral goodness, rather than the faults of people around you.

8. If there be any praise.... Think about the praiseworthy things — like the goodness and mercy of God, and His love — give praise to God with the fruit of righteousness produced by a Godly life.

Think on these things. Rest your mind on these things. You know, your mind is like the toy most of us had as children — a little rubber ball on a stretchy string, attached to a wooden paddle. It would go out in all directions but we could guide it back to that little wooden paddle. That's how your mind works. In the course of a day it goes out to a lot of different things and ideas. Not all of them are good or honest or of good report. But when your mind is at rest, when you realize where it's going — or already been — you need to guide it back to these eight behaviors God's Word gives us to discipline our mind. Put it to work thinking about things that are true...honest...just...pure...lovely...of good report...virtuous...praiseworthy.

Now, let's look at *II Corinthians 10:3-5* and then *Genesis 11:1-6* for a more detailed picture of what's going on in the invisible world of our mind — our natural man — where the battle for the future of man takes place.

> *"For though we walk in the flesh, we do not war after the flesh: (For the weapons of our warfare are not carnal, but mighty through God to the pulling down of strong holds;) Casting down imaginations, and every high thing that exalteth itself against the knowledge of God, and bringing into captivity every thought to the obedience of Christ."*

Keep in mind that phrase about "casting down imaginations" or getting control of our imaginations, and then let's look at the passage from *Genesis:*

> *"And the whole earth was of one language, and of one speech. And it came to pass, as they journeyed from the east, that they found a plain in the land of Shinar; and they dwelt there."*

> *"And they said one to another, Go to, let us make brick, and burn them thoroughly. And they had brick for stone, and slime had they for mortar."*

> *"And they said, Go to, let us build us a city and a tower whose top may reach unto heaven; and let us make us a name,*

*lest we be scattered abroad upon the face
of the whole earth."*

*"And the Lord came down to see the
city and the tower, which the children of
men builded. And the Lord said, Behold,
the people is one, and they have all one
language; and this they begin to do: and
now nothing will be restrained from
them, which they have imagined to do."*

Here God says *"nothing will be restrained from them
which they have imagined to do."* The word <u>imagined</u>
is related to the word <u>image</u>. What is an image but a
mental picture? We live our lives by mental pictures.
We imagine how things are and live with the mental
pictures we create of how things happen. And <u>why they
happen</u>.

The people written about in *Genesis 11* had a picture
in their minds of a tower reaching to heaven, a monu-
ment to themselves and their ingenuity. God saw that
they would accomplish it if He didn't slow them down.
They would have been worshipping themselves and their
ability, rather than God and His creative ability.

Likewise, we are propelled by the pictures we create
in our own mind. Everything we hear and see produces
an image — a mental picture. If I say that I have an apple
tree in my yard, it's easy enough for you to get a mental
picture of a somewhat gnarly old tree with red, yellow,
or green apples on it.

When Satan comes to us with destructive thoughts
and negative ideas, we immediately get those troubled,

destructive pictures in our mind as well. He might tell you the boss really doesn't like you and you are going to lose your job. Immediately, you get a picture of yourself with no job, losing your house, no food to put on the table for your family, standing in a handout line at the local charity in a snowstorm with bare feet.

This bombardment of good and evil thoughts and ideas into the mind is somewhat like the images before the lens of a camera. If I hold a camera in my hands and take pictures, it records whatever I focus into its eye. Its lens. Now, with a camera, I can focus the lens, take a picture, and then change my mind and not ever <u>see</u> that picture if I don't develop the film. I don't have to develop it and store the picture away forever and ever and look at it several times over. The camera has no memory of the event and won't ever see the scene again in that way unless I hold that picture up in front of its eye.

My mind — and yours — is continually taking pictures. Of course, these are automatically developed and filed away either in our subconscious mind (where they affect us without our realizing it) or in the conscious mind where we go through them several times a day. We control our conscious mind. We don't <u>have</u> to look at some of those images and ideas as often as we do...but frequently we <u>do</u> go through that box of depressing ideas — those memories of tragic failures or missed opportunities — Satan has deposited there just waiting for us to sift through. Of course, God has made available to us a whole Bible full of stories and examples of His love that we can file away on top of the painful things Satan would like to show us. We can see our faults and failures through the filter of His love and encouragement and grace.

90

No wonder the Bible tells us about the power of the mind and our imagination in *II Corinthians 10:5*, that we should be busy *"Casting down imaginations, and every high thing that exalteth itself against the knowledge of God, and bringing into captivity every thought to the obedience of Christ."* We need to put a fence around our imaginations and our behaviors that would not bring honor to our Lord.

Every day of our lives we desperately need to ask the Holy Spirit to set a guard over our thought life.

> *Thoughts become words;*
> *Words become actions;*
> *Actions become habits;*
> *Habits become character;*
> *Character becomes destiny.*

When we fail, whether it's seven or seventy times seven failures a day, we need to be quick to bring that failure to God. In a sincere spirit of repentance we need to ask God to help us kick the carnal man and his sinful source right out of the driver's seat of our life and turn those controls back to spirit man on the double. Like the rubber ball on the end of the string, we need re-directed and brought back to the paddle, the source of our energy.

When we make this our pattern for "deprogramming" and "reprogramming," we have a fresh understanding of and appreciation for Scriptures like these...

> *"Seven times a day do I praise thee be-*
> *cause of thy righteous judgements. Great*

peace have they which love thy law; and nothing shall offend them" (Psalms 119:164,165).

"Peace I leave with you, my peace I give unto you: not as the world giveth, give I unto you. Let not your heart be troubled, neither let it be afraid" (John 14:27).

"And the peace of God, which passeth all understanding, shall keep your hearts and minds through Christ Jesus" (Philippians 4:7).

"For to be carnally minded is death: but to be spiritually minded is life and peace" (Romans 8:6).

"And let the peace of God rule in your hearts, to the which also ye are called in one body; and be ye thankful" (Colossians 3:15).

Chapter 8
"It is Finished!"

As we begin the final chapter of this book, which deals with the spirit man, let's take a close look at *Romans 8:8-10* as it appears in The Amplified Bible:

> *"So then those who are living the life of the flesh — catering to the appetites and impulses of their carnal nature — cannot please or satisfy God, or be acceptable to Him."*

> *"But you are not living the life of the flesh, you are living the life of the Spirit, if the (Holy) Spirit of God (really) dwells within you — directs and controls you. But if any one does not possess the (Holy) Spirit of Christ, he is none of His — he does not belong to Christ (is not truly a child of God)."*

> *"But if Christ lives in you, (then al-*
> *though your natural) body is dead by*
> *reason of sin and guilt, the spirit is alive*
> *because of (the) righteousness (that He*
> *imputes to you)."*

Now, let's look at *Genesis 1:26-30* in the King James translation of the Bible:

> *"And God said, Let us make man in*
> *our image, after our likeness: and let*
> *them have dominion over the fish of the*
> *sea, and over the fowl of the air, and over*
> *the cattle, and over all the earth, and over*
> *every creeping thing that creepeth upon*
> *the earth."*

> *"So God created man in his own image,*
> *in the image of God created he him; male*
> *and female created he them. And God*
> *blessed them, and God said unto them,*
> *Be fruitful, and multiply, and replenish*
> *the earth, and subdue it: and have domin-*
> *ion over the fish of the sea, and over the*
> *fowl of the air, and over every living thing*
> *that moveth upon the earth."*

> *"And God said, Behold, I have given*
> *you every herb-bearing seed, which is*
> *upon the face of all the earth, and every*
> *tree, in the which is the fruit of a tree*
> *yielding seed; to you it shall be for meat.*

*And to every beast of the earth, and to
every fowl of the air, and to every thing
that creepeth upon the earth, wherein
there is life, I have given every green herb
for meat: and it was so."*

From these verses, we realize that man lives in a physical body and he is designed to be very conscious of the
physical, natural world around him. The natural, physical,
man is very conscious of and tied to his physical sur-
roundings. God established that in Eden.

Because the natural, physical, human man (or woman)
is the "continental divide" of the spirit world's communi-
cations and influence on our life, he is constantly receiving messages from both God and Satan. David experienced this regularly, and wrote much about it in his
Psalms. Let's look at just a few references:

*"Why art thou cast down, O my soul?
and why art thou disquieted in me? hope
thou in God: for I shall yet praise him
for the help of his countenance...O my
God, my soul is cast down within me...
Weeping may endure for a night, but joy
cometh in the morning...He healeth the
broken in heart, and bindeth up their
wounds" (Psalm 42; Psalm 30; Psalm
147).*

David's natural man was frequently depressed, and at
the same time he was filled with anxiety and apprehen-
sion. No doubt today he would have taken an "upper"
for his depression and a "downer" for his anxiety and

hoped they would meet somewhere in the middle and give him relief.

David helps us understand that not only is man a physical, natural being, conscious of the world around him that he can see and know with his senses, but he is also a soul, conscious of himself. Because man is also a spirit, he is capable of being conscious of God. He can communicate with God and the spirit world. *Proverbs 20:27* tells us, *"The spirit of man is the candle of the Lord, searching all the inward parts of the belly."* And *Psalm 18:28* tells us, *"For thou wilt light my candle: the Lord my God will enlighten my darkness."*

If the spirit of man is the candle of the Lord, then when the Lord lights our candle He is lighting — or enlightening — our spirit. How does He do this? *Job 3:28* tells us, *"But there is a spirit in man: and the inspiration of the Almighty giveth them understanding."* The inspiration of the Almighty to our spirit man is like touching the flame to an unlit candle. It is then, after His spirit has enlightened our spirit, that the spirit man within man knows God...believes God...understands God. The inspiration of the Almighty to our spirit man brings an understanding of himself to us. One New Testament writer, at least, used this analogy to describe Christ's mission on earth: *"To give light to them that sit in darkness"* (Luke 2:79).

Now let's look at how these three parts of man fit together in proper order. Let's read *I Thessalonians 5:23 "And the very God of peace sanctify you wholly; and I pray God your whole spirit and soul and body be preserved blameless unto the coming of our Lord Jesus Christ."* Notice the order of those words: spirit, and soul, and body.

96

Why did the Holy Ghost instruct Paul to say these words in this particular order? Why not <u>body</u>, then <u>soul</u>, and then <u>spirit</u>? Because He wanted the chain of command to be right. You see, before Adam sinned the chain of command was spirit, soul, and body. Because his spirit man was in control, Adam was creative enough to give names to everything God created. He even named his wife. Let's read about this in *Genesis 2:19-23.*

> *"And out of the ground the Lord God formed every beast of the field, and every fowl of the air; and brought them unto Adam to see what he would call them: and whatsoever Adam called every living creature, that was the name thereof."*

> *"And Adam gave names to all cattle, and to the fowl of the air, and to every beast of the field; but for Adam there was not found an helpmeet for him. And the Lord God caused a deep sleep to fall upon Adam, and he slept: and he took one of his ribs, and closed up the flesh instead thereof. And the rib, which the Lord God had taken from man, made he a woman, and brought her unto the man."*

> *"And Adam said, This is now bone of my bones, and flesh of my flesh: she shall be called Woman, because she was taken out of Man."*

Before the fall, Adam's wife was simply named

97

"Woman" but that was not an appropriate name for her after the fall. The chain of command had been changed — tampered with — and Adam had to rename her. The order of command was now body, soul, and then spirit. "Eve" became the carnal name for Adam's mate. However, the day is coming soon when the chain of command will be set completely right again, and we who are born again Christians will also have a new name. *Revelation 2:17* tells us, *"To him that overcometh will I give to eat of the hidden manna, and will give him a white stone, and in the stone a new name written, which no man knoweth saving he that receiveth it."* In that day, our old carnal name will not suffice; we will have a new name. Praise God!

In *Genesis 2:15-17,* God had told man that he could eat of every tree of the garden except the tree of the knowledge of good and evil. God warned man that in that day when he ate of this special tree, he would surely die.

Now, we know that man did not die physically that day. The Scripture tells us that Adam lived to the ripe old age of 930 years. It was Adam's spirit man who died in the garden that day, and his soul became separated from God. God's ordained chain of command was reversed. Carnal man got in the driver's seat of Adam's life. Adam held the door open wide and said to carnal man, "Come on in! Set yerself down. Let's talk awhile."

Almost immediately, Adam and Eve began to search out ways to cover their sins and restore themselves to fellowship with the Creator. When Cain was born, Eve declared, "I have gotten a man from the Lord." She thought this was the promised redeemer to be sent from God. She thought Cain would fulfill that promise and bring them back to the condition they were in before the fall, when they enjoyed close communion and fellowship with God.

Instead of a deliverer, Cain turned out to be a rabble rouser and murderer. Eve's second son was named "Abel", meaning "a breath of fresh air." Cain had turned out to be something of a disappointment, and Eve thought surely this man-child would be the one. But before long Abel was dead and Cain was a fugitive. Why? The chain of command was in the wrong order.

Look at what happened in David's life when spirit man was not in control. In his prayer of repentance after he had committed adultery and murder, he said to God, *"Against thee, and thee only, have I sinned and done this evil in thy sight."* He wasn't quite telling the truth. He had not only sinned against God, but against Bathsheba, against her husband (Uriah), his own family, and the entire nation of Israel.

David tried to find an excuse for his sin by saying, in the same verse, *"that thou mightest be justified when thou speakest, and be clear when thou judgest" (Psalm 51:4).* God didn't need David to sin so that He could be justified and Israel could see Him deliver clear and just punishment only to the exact offender. A just and merciful God doesn't need public justification and wouldn't order such a destructive scenario just to prove He could hit the right person with appropriate punishment.

In verse 5, David even tried to lay the blame for his sin on his mother. *"Behold,"* he said, *"I was shapen in iniquity; and in sin did my mother conceive me."* His carnal man was alive and well and trying — as usual — to put the blame for his behavior on someone else.

David presents a clear picture of the natural man being

in control and caught in sin. *"Hide thy face from my sins,"* he prayed in *Psalm 51:9.* He wanted God to over-look his wrong doing.

But just a little bit later, we get the beautiful contrast of spirit man restored. *"Create in me a clean heart, O God: and renew a right spirit within me. Cast me not away from thy presence; and take not thy holy spirit from me. Restore unto me the joy of thy salvation; and uphold me with thy free spirit."*

Now the spirit man was talking. He didn't come before God to defend his case or try to make someone else responsible for his sin. He just came to plead guilty and seek forgiveness.

Psalm 51:13, then, gives us a beautiful picture of what the <u>natural man</u> does when the spirit man is in control. *"Then will I teach transgressors thy ways; and sinners shall be converted unto thee."* In verse 14 and 15 we read what the <u>carnal man</u> will do when the spirit man is in control. *"...And my tongue shall sing aloud of thy righteousness. O Lord, open thou my lips; and my mouth shall shew forth thy praise."* *Psalm 51:17* tells us, finally, what the <u>spirit man</u> is like when God is in control of him. *"The sacrifices of God are a broken spirit: a broken and a contrite heart, O God, thou wilt not despise."*

As we bring this chapter and this book to a close, I want us to take a look at Jesus and at the battle that raged within Him as He faced the cross.

"And being in an agony he prayed more earnestly: and his sweat was as it were great drops of blood falling down to the ground." Notice that in this verse, *Luke 22:44,* He sweat not drops of actual blood, but *"as it were"* drops of blood, or something like blood. Now,

100

blood and water in the human body mix only when the heart ruptures. Jesus' great heart had already begun to rupture; the blood and water in His body had started to mix. His carnal man (because He was totally human) and spirit man (because He was totally divine) were about to engage in the battle of all eternity. The intensity of that battle ruptured his heart. Let's look at the event as it unfolded:

> *"Then cometh Jesus with them unto a place called Gethsemane, and saith unto the disciples, Sit ye here, while I go and pray yonder. And he took with him Peter and the two sons of Zebedee, and began to be sorrowful and very heavy. Then saith he unto them, My soul is exceeding sorrowful, even unto death: tarry ye here, and watch with me" (Matthew 26:36-38).*

Notice in verse 38 He says, *"My soul (my mind, my natural man) is exceeding sorrowful, even unto death."* The battle was raging in His natural man. He knew what He was facing and His flesh and mind didn't want to go through with it. No doubt He had seen Roman crucifixions, and other forms of Roman justice. The trial, the beating, and the crucifixion, were horrible ordeals.

I used to believe and preach that Jesus took 39 stripes, but that is not the case. Thirty-nine stripes were the number of blows that Jewish law would let one Jew inflict upon another, but Jesus wasn't beaten by Jews. He was beaten and crucified by the Romans. Roman law then said that a Roman soldier could beat a prisoner with as many stripes as he wanted to inflict.

Many prisoners died from this initial beating, because the Roman soldiers were such masterful torturers. They would tie a prisoner to a post, then take up a whip called a <u>cat o' nine tails</u> with nine pieces of leather attached to one handle. Shreds of bone, metal, and broken pottery were woven into these nine pieces of leather.

As the soldier started to beat the prisoner, he would start about the top of the ear. As he brought his whip down it would wrap around the face, and the pieces of bone and metal would dig into the flesh. When the soldier pulled the handle, the flesh was ripped and cut to ribbons. Often the eyes would be pulled out of their sockets, and left dangling upon the cheekbone. The soldier would slowly work his way down the body of the victim to the small of the back, then he would start on the other side and do the same, crisscrossing the body all the way down. By the time he had finished, the torso was in shreds with the rib cage and vital organs exposed. It was easy for the Roman soldier to pierce the heart of Jesus with one plunge of his spear, because he could most likely see it beating between His ribs.

We see beautiful paintings of Jesus stretched out, with a drop of blood or two spilling down, and a few faint lash marks on His body. A painting that accurately depicted what He endured would be too graphic for most of us to look at even for an instant. The Roman soldiers nailed their victims to the cross in a squatting position, so the intestines would be pushed up into the chest cavity, making it almost impossible to breathe. The only way the victim could take a breath would be to lift the weight of his body on the nails in his hands and feet, take a breath, and slump back down.

Imagine with me, Jesus hanging on the cross. His heart

has long since ruptured from the strain of having to take our vile sins into His pure body...all the filth of the rotten deeds of mankind over thousands of years \of murder...child abuse...robbery...lies...deceptions...as He hangs there, He finds the strength to pull His body up enough to give himself breath and says to the Father, *"Father, forgive them; for they know not what they do."* We read also, in *Luke 23:46, "And when Jesus had cried with a loud voice, he said, Father, into thy hands I commend my spirit: and having said thus, he gave up the ghost."* His spirit man was in control — still — after all He had endured.

Finally, let's look at *I Thessalonians 5:23,24* one more time.

> *"And the very God of peace sanctify you wholly; and I pray God your whole spirit and soul and body be preserved blameless unto the coming of our Lord Jesus Christ. Faithful is he that calleth you, who also will do it."*

The battle rages, and we may lose a battle here and there, but with God's help we will win the war. When we have learned who our enemy is, and how he comes against us, when we have learned how to use the Word of God to fight the enemy...in short, when we have learned the power available to us once we put spirit man in the driver's seat of our lives, and the chain of command is in order, we can have the peace of God and be victorious. We can say that though emotions were once our master and circumstances our Lord, praise God the Lord of our emotions and the Lord of our circumstances is now in control. Life will never be the same!

FLESHLY, CARNAL MAN
RULED BY FIVE SENSES
FEELINGS IS HIS VOICE

NATURAL, SOULISH MAN
REASON IS HIS VOICE

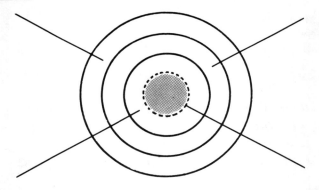

SPIRIT MAN
CONSCIENCE IS HIS VOICE

HOLY SPIRIT
VOICE OF GOD

CHART #1

ISAIAH 45:7

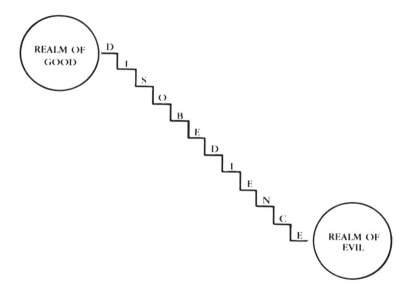

CHART #2

GENESIS 1:26, 27

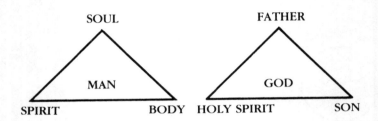

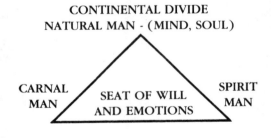

CHART #3

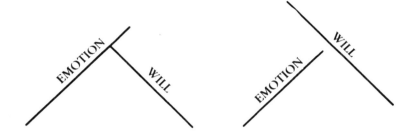

CHART #4

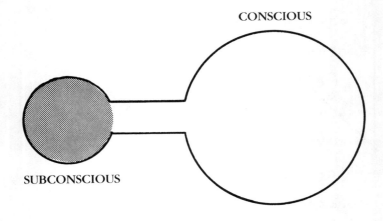

CHART #5

Dear Reader,

It is my prayer that, if you do not know Jesus Christ as your personal Savior, you will accept Him now. For your benefit, I have written the following prayer:

"Lord Jesus, I come to you now, confessing that I am a sinner. I ask you to forgive me of all my sins. Wash me in your blood; come into my heart. I accept you now as my Lord and Savior and I confess with my mouth that, according to Your Word, I am saved.

Thank you, Jesus.

If you have accepted Christ, please write your name below together with the date and time, and keep it for your personal record.

Name_____

Date_____ Time_____

Epilogue

For many years I was angry with the world because I thought the world was mistreating me. Everyone else seemed to have it so much better and easier than I did. I was angry with God because He didn't give me a choice as to whether or not I wanted to be born into this world. I felt that He had forced life with all its miseries on me. I was angry with my father for mistreating and abusing my mother and all of us children. Last of all, I was angry with myself because I couldn't make heads or tails out of life. I had a terrible self image, always feeling like I was worthless and no one cared.

But Someone did care — and over a period of some twenty years He revealed Himself and His love to me, so patiently, in so many ways. God used the little things of everyday life such as the song of a bird, the delicate beauty of a daisy, the laughing trickle of a brook tumbling over the rocks, or the smile of a friend. How often did I see the love of God in my precious wife and children!

Not all at once, like a magician pulling a rabbit out of a hat, but little by little God taught me the principles I have talked about in this book. He showed me that there are no magic formulas for life, but by applying these principles to our daily living we can live a happy, victorious life. No longer do I flounder in a sea of anger, bitterness and resentment. I live each day to the full enjoying a life of peace, joy and contentment.

My prayer is that after reading this book you will begin applying these principles to your daily life, checking up to see who is in the driver's seat of YOUR life. You will begin to experience not only peace <u>with</u> God, but also the peace <u>of</u> God.

ORDER BLANK

Please mail or deliver to me _____ copies of *Renew Your Mind,* at a per copy price of $5.95 plus $2.00 for postage and handling. I enclose my check for $_____ payable to J C Publishing Company, P.O. Box 3117, Baton Rouge, Louisiana 70821, phone (504) 293-2842.

Send copies to:

Name_____

Address_____

City, state and zip_____

ORDER BLANK

Please mail or deliver to me _____ copies of *Renew Your Mind,* at a per copy price of $5.95 plus $2.00 for postage and handling. I enclose my check for $_____ payable to J C Publishing Company, P.O. Box 3117, Baton Rouge, Louisiana 70821, phone (504) 293-2842.

Send copies to:

Name_____

Address_____

City, state and zip_____